cpuelii

British Columbia

AN ILLUSTRATED HISTORY

REVISED AND UPDATED

British Columbia

AN ILLUSTRATED HISTORY

GEOFFREY MOLYNEUX

RAINCOAST BOOKS

Vancouver

Raincoast Books acknowledges the ongoing financial support of the Government of Canada through The Canada Council for the Arts and the Book Publishing Industry Development Program (BPIDP); and the Government of British Columbia through the BC Arts Council.

Text design by Jacqueline Verkley

National Library of Canada Cataloguing in Publication Data

Molyneux, Geoffrey.
  British Columbia

  Includes bibliographical references and index.
  ISBN 1-55192-420-X

  1. British Columbia—History. 2. British Columbia—History—Pictorial works. I. Title.
FC3811.M64 2001 971.1   C2001-910849-4   F1088.M64 2001

Raincoast Books
9050 Shaughnessy Street
Vancouver, British Columbia
Canada, V6P 6E5
www.raincoast.com

Printed and bound in Canada.
1 2 3 4 5 6 7 8 9 10

Contents

Preface

This book makes no claims to being a complete or academic history of British Columbia; its contents are closer to journalism — telling the story, in simple language, of events whose impact changed people's lives.

You'll find stories about how men, women and children lived in a land full of promise and danger, on the shore of an ocean equally fertile and perilous. Then the stories tell how British Columbians built cities and factories, logged the forests, fished the ocean, dug the mines and traded with the world. As society became more complicated, political questions became paramount, and so the stories tell how British Columbians chose the politicians who would run their lives.

You'll also find photographs, maps, graphics, anecdotes and intriguing snippets. And, at the end of each chapter there's an excerpt from a work by an author of the period.

Where did it all come from? Books, newspapers, magazines, broadcasts, websites and gossip. Many of the books and websites consulted are listed at the end of the book with a short note about their contents.

This is a revised and updated edition of *British Columbia: An Illustrated History*, first published in 1992. Some stories of the early years have been updated with new information. The first edition gave only a brief mention of Bill Vander Zalm, the last of the Socred premiers, and his successor, the NDP's Mike Harcourt. This new edition describes the dramatic changes that have occurred in the government of this province since the publication of the first edition: the triumphs and failures of Vander Zalm, Harcourt and his fellow NDP premiers, Glen Clark and Ujjal Dosanjh. It ends with the story of Liberal leader Gordon Campbell's annihilation of the provincial NDP and the consequences of his party's victory.

— *G. M.* —

ONE

10,000 BC TO 1871

Winds of Change

The life of the First Nations peoples of the coast — the Haida, Tsimshian, Kwakiutl, Nuu-chah-nulth and Coast Salish — seems to have changed when the sea level stopped fluctuating around 5,000 years ago. As sea shores and river deltas developed, fish and shellfish became easier to catch and preserve for later use. Now people had time for doing more than just gathering food; they began building and decorating homes, weaving, making boats of cedar, and tools and weapons of bone and stone. Life was harder for the people of the Interior — the Sekani, the Dene-thah (Slavey), Dunne-za (Beaver), Dakelh (Carrier), Tsilhqot'in (Chilcotin), Secwepemc (Shuswap), Tahltan, Kaska, Nlaka'pamux (Thompson), St'at'imx (Lillooet), Okanagan and Kutenai (Kootenay) — where food was harder to get and the climate harsher.

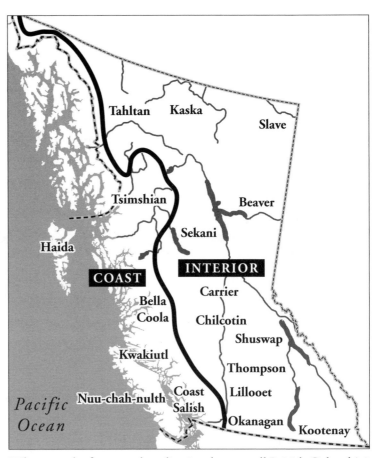

Who were the first people to live in what we call British Columbia? Where did they come from and what kind of folk were they?

No one knows the precise answers to these questions, but most experts agree that the first people to live in Canada arrived some time during the last Ice Age. It seems these first migrants came from Asia over a strip of land now covered by the Bering Sea. Through a corridor that ran between the ice masses and south-southeast along the east side of what are now the Rockies, they slowly moved to what is now the Midwest of the United States. As the ice receded they began to head north, and about 11,500 years ago, people were living in parts of what is now British Columbia.

We know this because archaeologists digging in a pit near Fort St. John have found stone tools, weapons and carved bison bones that they say are 11,500 years old. The people who left these pieces of evidence lived in tents or caves and hunted bison and other animals. It seems safe to assume that similar bands of hunters and their families were roaming the uplands of central British Columbia around that time. About 7,000 years ago, these people of the Interior began to move into the river valleys and fish for salmon. They started to build homes excavated into the ground and to use tools archaeologists call microblades, primitive razor blades chipped from rock by artisans.

The Pacific coast of B.C. does not fit neatly into this pattern, however. The people who lived on the coast and along the rivers close to the sea seem to have had other roots. They used tools different from those used in the Interior. Perhaps they were descendants of a group that came over the Bering Bridge much later; perhaps they came south by sea. There's little doubt, though, that people have been living on the coast for more than 9,000 years. We know this from diggings at Namu, on the mainland coast just north of Vancouver Island, and at Lawn Point, on Graham Island in the Queen Charlottes. But we should be cautious: these kinds of estimates, discoveries and analyses change as new finds are made and technology gets better.

The life led by these coastal people changed rapidly when the sealevel stopped fluctuating 5,000 to 6,000 years ago. The coastline became more permanent, and river deltas and tidal flats developed. Fish and shellfish became much easier to catch and harvest; settlements grew and population increased. Now fish could be stored by drying or smoking on the shore, and this left time for activities other than gathering food. Men and women developed the skills and tools to build homes and boats, make nets, weave clothes and make harpoons, fish hooks, knives and weapons from bone and stone. Trade routes opened to the

This portrait of Chief Maquinna of the Mowachaht, a First Nation of the Nuu-chah-nulth (Nootka) people, was drawn in 1791 by Tomas Suria. Because all Mowachaht chiefs take the same name, it's not known if this is the Maquinna who greeted James Cook and the Spanish, traded furs with the British and Americans, allegedly gave land to the rascally British captain John Meares and later attacked the trading vessel Boston, *killing most of its crew and capturing ship's armourer John Jewitt and sailmaker John Thompson.*

Interior, and exotic objects such as personal jewellery and decorated housewares, as well as mundane products like eulachon oil, were exchanged for hides and food.

Around 2,500 years ago, the people in the Fraser delta, the central mainland coast, northern Vancouver Island and in the Queen Charlottes and Prince Rupert areas had developed a social system with elaborate rituals, a spiritual life and an artistic tradition. Their economic system, perfectly suited to their environment, supplied them with food, clothes, homes and weapons. Archaeological diggings in the Fraser Valley, Cache Creek, Kamloops and Crowsnest Pass areas show communities leading similar but probably less elaborate lives.

The Nootka (today Nuu-chah-nulth) people of northern Vancouver Island were the first in B.C. to spend some time with Europeans. These European explorers, scientists and traders came from societies eager to learn about new worlds and claim territory for their leaders, and they wrote books and reports and drew sketches about the people they met, people who seemed strange and exotic. And so we know a good deal about the life led by the Nootka in the late 18th century.

They seem to have cultivated few plants, but their supply of meat was abundant: fish, shellfish, deer, elk, bear, goat, seal, porpoise and whale were all part of their diet. Fish, chiefly salmon, was eaten raw, broiled, boiled or smoked. Hooks, rakes and nets were made from wood and plant fibre.

The men built homes from large planks and posts, designed so that they could be erected quickly when family groups moved between their inland winter homes and summer camps on the coast. Here, starting in early spring, they could catch the first herring and salmon.

While fishing, they watched out to sea for whales, and the first sightings prompted dancing and celebration. The chief led the hunters, who used harpoons made of bone with bladders tied to them to slow the wounded whale and to show its position. The chief's wife had to lie motionless in bed at home during the hunt,

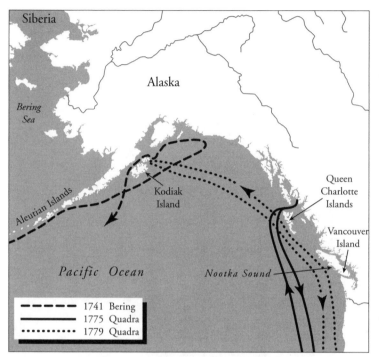

Siberia

Alaska

Bering
Sea

Aleutian Islands

Kodiak
Island

Queen
Charlotte
Islands

Vancouver
Island

Pacific Ocean

Nootka Sound

- - - - - 1741 Bering
————— 1775 Quadra
••••••• 1779 Quadra

*Exploring the Pacific Coast.
Vitus Bering, a Dane working for the Russians, confirmed in 1729 that a broad
stretch of water — now
called the Bering Strait —
separated Asia and America.
He explored the American
North Pacific coast in
1740–41 to a latitude of 55
degrees north, but died of
scurvy during the voyage.*

The Spanish frigate
Santiago, *commanded by
Juan Hernandez, sailed
from Mexico, reached the
Queen Charlottes and
traded with the Haida in
1774. In 1775, the Spanish
sailed north again. This
time the* Santiago *was
accompanied by the* Sonora,
*commanded by Juan de la
Bodega y Quadra (who
negotiated with Captain
George Vancouver 17 years
later). Quadra reached 57
degrees north. He sailed
north again as a member of
an expedition in 1779 and
reached 60 degrees.*

for if she moved, the people believed, the whale would move, too, and escape.

The men burned out the insides of large trees to build canoes, and developed tools of stone and bone to split and fashion the cedar they found around them. While the men fished and hunted, the women gathered shellfish, prepared and preserved the food and wove clothes from cedar bark. They also made the nets for fishing and the mats for the communal homes. Inside the homes were fire-places, sleeping compartments and storage boxes for furs and cloaks. Some had a small room believed to be a kind of chapel.

Family groups consisted of people related by ancestry, through either male or female lines. Most property, such as land, homes or fishing sites, belonged to one of these groups or its leader. The group used captives, taken in battle or raids, as slaves.

The lot of children and women was not happy. Children were sometimes sold and enslaved; women had virtually no choice in

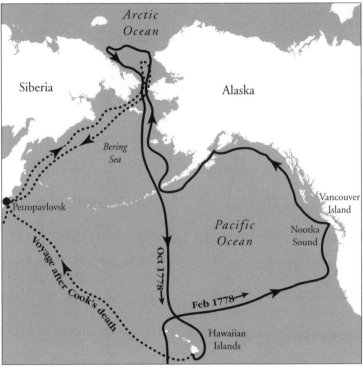

Yorkshireman James Cook was born in 1728, served with the Royal Navy at Louisbourg, Nova Scotia, in 1758 and surveyed the St. Lawrence near Quebec for General James Wolfe in 1759. In 1768–71 and 1772–75 he sailed around the world, exploring and mapping parts of Australia, New Zealand, Antarctica and the islands of the South Pacific. In 1776 Cook left England with orders to find the Northwest Passage from the Pacific. He stopped at the Sandwich Islands (Hawaii) and reached the Pacific coast on March 7, 1778. Bad weather forced him to sail well out to sea as he sailed north; he may be excused, then, for missing the mouth...

marriage and were expected to be monogamous. But women were not necessarily submissive and weak: some early traders reported that aboriginal men were abused and beaten by women for failing to get a good price for skins. Female slaves and lower-class women were used as drudges, prostitutes for visitors (such as the Europeans) or bed partners.

The winds and tides that brought these Pacific coast people their food and warm, wet climate also brought massive changes. Europeans, driven by the desire for wealth, power, knowledge and the perceived need to bring the salvation of Christianity to unfortunate Native people, had started sailing into the Pacific from the south in the 16th century. Among them was Queen Elizabeth's favourite buccaneer and explorer, Sir Francis Drake, who sailed up the California coast in 1576. Legends about his landfalls farther up the coast — including one in what is now British Columbia

— have tickled the fancies of amateur historians but have found little support so far from professionals.

First Nations people told the Europeans about strange visitors from across the sea — probably Japan or Hawaii — and of ships wrecked at sea or on the coast. Perhaps these are the sources of the iron tools and baubles made of metals found locally. An Asian urn, 300 years old, was found by a fishboat close to the Strait of Juan de Fuca in 1979.

Russian traders reached the northern Pacific in the 1600s. (They were still trading there when Russia sold Alaska to the United States in 1867.) In 1741 their countryman, Vitus Bering, who had discovered the Bering Sea 12 years earlier, explored large tracts of the North Pacific. There is, however, no firm evidence of foreign ships reaching the coast of what would become British Columbia until late in the 18th century. First came the Spanish, sailing north from Mexico. In 1774 they met the Haida off the Queen Charlottes and later, driven south by storms, sought shelter in what we now call Nootka Sound. They don't seem to have come ashore.

Two years later, on July 12, 1776, Captain James Cook sailed from Plymouth in the west of England in the 420-ton *Resolution*, ahead of his other ship, *Discovery*. In early 1778 he was in the North Pacific and came upon some islands he named for his powerful patron, the fourth Earl of Sandwich; they are now the Hawaiian Islands. Cook was riding a crest of fame after two successful voyages of exploration to Australia, New Zealand, the south Pacific and Antarctica. This time his orders from the Admiralty told him to look for the Northwest Passage, which had eluded explorers searching from the Atlantic side.

On February 2, 1778, Cook left Hawaii, beating before the wind toward the coast that was the last stretch of land in the world's temperate zones still unexplored by Europeans. On March 7, using a new chronometer — an accurate watch that helped him determine longitude — and the other navigational aids provided by the Admiralty (aids only recently supplanted by

... of the Columbia River and the Strait of Juan de Fuca. (Captain George Vancouver, 14 years later, did little better; he also missed the Columbia and had no excuses.) After a stay in Friendly Cove on Vancouver Island, Cook sailed north into the Bering Sea to find the Northwest Passage, but heavy ice forced him to turn back to winter in the Sandwich Islands. There he was killed in a squabble on February 14, 1779.

Captain Cook's chronometer, which he called a watch and took on his second and third great voyages, helped him determine the longitude (east-west direction) of his ship. Named K1, it was made by Larcum Kendall in 1769 and was a very accurate copy of the first chronometer made by inventor John Harrison. After Cook's ships returned to England, K1 was used in the first surveys of New South Wales.

radar and satellite navigation), *Resolution* and *Discovery* came to the coast of the Pacific Northwest at 44 degrees 33 minutes north latitude — central Oregon. Gales forced Cook and the *Resolution*'s master and navigator, William Bligh, of *Bounty* fame, to sail up the uncharted coast well out to sea for three weeks, even though they were running short of water and needed to repair *Resolution*'s masts. As a result, they missed the mouth of the Columbia River and the Strait of Juan de Fuca. At four in the afternoon on March 29, through a break in the weather, the ships sighted a gap in the coastline and edged their way into the inlet we now call Friendly Cove, in Nootka Sound.

Cook and his ships stayed in Nootka until April 26. His men included around 200 seamen, blacksmiths, artificers, carpenters, an artist, an astrologer and a surgeon, led by 20 officers, including George Vancouver, who was to return later. They set up an observatory, explored the inlet, repaired their rotting masts and traded knick-knacks and pieces of metal — anything from nails to buttons and pewter plates — for sea-otter furs. The goats and sheep on board were tethered ashore to crop fresh grass and bushes.

Everyone got on well together: there was no brutal conquest by an invading force. The seeds of decay had been sown, however. Disease and a foreign set of values were to disrupt a society that had evolved over thousands of years.

Cook sailed north from Nootka to continue his search for the Northwest Passage. When his men next touched land — in Russian territory — they found that the furs they had bought for plates or buttons were worth hundreds of pounds. News of the fortunes to be made on the Pacific Northwest coast reached the Far East, England and Europe, and by the mid-1780s other ships, mostly American, were busy trading with First Nations people for sea-otter furs. One of these, sailing under the Austrian flag to avoid British licensing laws, was commanded by Charles Barkley. He brought along his 18-year-old, red-haired bride, Frances — the first known European woman to visit British Columbia — and her Hawaiian maid.

The sea-otter fur trade, in which First Nations people worked with the Americans who soon dominated the British Columbia coast, was the first of exploitative hunts. After the sea otters, it was the turn of fur seals, then whales and salmon and other food fish. It took about 100 years before conservation could take effect.

All this activity revived Spanish interest in Nootka, and in May 1789, the Spanish started to build a fort close to the shore. To assert their sovereignty over the area, they captured some of the men working for John Meares, a renegade British captain and trader who claimed that, a year before, Chief Maquinna of the Nootka's Mowachaht First Nation had granted him land and the right to build a trading post. Meares went to England, raved about the treachery and arrogance of the Spanish and persuaded the British government to devote £2 million for war with Spain. But diplomacy won the day. After all, the Revolution in France, just across the English Channel, was bigger stuff than events in a tiny inlet thousands of kilometres away. Britain and Spain signed the Nootka Convention in October 1790, and Spain seemed to have dropped its claim to sovereignty over the Pacific Northwest. Meares got his men back.

This was still unknown territory, and both Britain and Spain decided to do more exploring and to name envoys who could meet and settle the local dispute. Spain named Don Juan Francisco de la Bodega y Quadra; Britain assigned Captain George Vancouver, who had sailed to Nootka with Cook. Both eminently reasonable fellows, Quadra and Vancouver cooperated in mapping the coast, inshore passages and inlets, including Burrard Inlet. Then, after meeting at Nootka, they agreed to disagree and let their governments work things out. After two years of exploration and mapping, Vancouver left for home, where he was persecuted by a renegade officer he had punished on the voyage to the Pacific coast. Vancouver died in 1798. A revised Nootka Convention was signed the same year, and Spain effectively dropped claims to the Pacific Northwest. From now on it was a tussle between British and American fur traders, on sea and land, with Russia playing a minor, spoiling role.

Captain George Vancouver served with Captain Cook as a 15-year-old midshipman on Cook's great 1772–75 voyage and expedition to the Pacific Northwest in 1776–79. In April 1792, Vancouver was back in B.C. waters, charged with settling the Nootka dispute with Spain and with mapping the coast leading to the Northwest Passage. Before returning to England, Vancouver mapped Puget Sound, Georgia Strait, Burrard Inlet and much of Vancouver Island. He died in England in May 1798.

ABOVE: Alexander Mackenzie reached the Pacific overland while Captain Vancouver's men were still mapping the coast. Mackenzie created what is probably the first graffiti on the Pacific coast: on a rock at Bella Coola he wrote in grease coloured with vermilion: "Alex Mackenzie from Canada by land 22nd July 1793."

RIGHT: Routes and forts of the fur traders: these explorers looked for land and water routes, a good supply of furs and sites for settlements, often optimistically called forts.

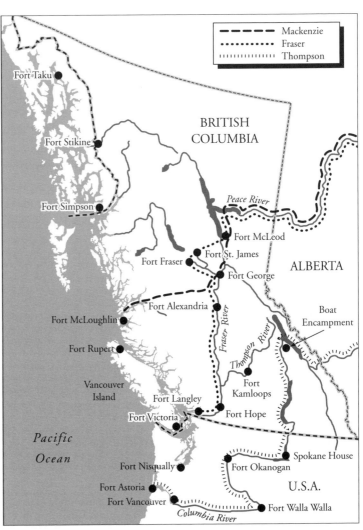

While Yankee and Russian traders and Spanish and British navy officers were jostling for position on the coast, the great land explorers were probing the Interior for the British-controlled fur trade. The North West Company, a loosely knit group of fur traders competing with the Hudson's Bay Company, sent Alexander Mackenzie, Simon Fraser and David Thompson to find new sources of furs, open trading posts and blaze routes to the Pacific.

Mackenzie failed in his first try to reach the Pacific overland and ended up on the bleak Arctic shoreline. He went back to England, learned surveying and astronomy and tried again. On July 22, 1793, after following Native trails and listening to the advice of helpful Native men and women, he reached the Pacific Ocean near Bella Coola. But the trails he followed hardly made a good route for the fur trade.

Then it was Simon Fraser's turn. In 1775 the Spanish had seen the mouth of a massive river flowing into the Pacific around 46 degrees north latitude. Both Cook and Vancouver had sailed past the mouth without noticing it. In 1792 an American fur trader, Robert Gray, had sailed into the river and named it for his ship, the *Columbia*. In 1805 Americans Meriwether Lewis and William Clark, leading a government-sponsored expedition overland, reached the mouth of the Columbia and planted the United States flag. Fraser's task, then, was to find a route through New Caledonia (central B.C.) to the mouth of the Columbia. In the spring of 1808, he canoed down streams and torrents, hacked his way through the bush, clung to cliffs and at last sailed into the estuary of what was later called the Fraser River. But the Native people of the estuary, the Musqueam, were none too friendly and,

Nine years after Captain Cook left Friendly Cove, the first European woman reached what was to become British Columbia. She was 18-year-old Frances Barkley, who had married Captain Charles Barkley a year earlier in Ostend, Belgium. She then sailed with him on a trading voyage to North America.

She lived in a tiny cabin next to her husband's. They reached the west coast of Vancouver Island in 1787, then left later for Alaska and China to sell the hundreds of sea-otter pelts they had bought. Her first son was born a year later.

After a two-year rest in England, Frances and her husband sailed again on another worldwide trading voyage. In 1794 they settled in England, where Frances died in 1854.

She bore seven children, some while at sea. Four survived to marry and give her grandchildren.

The paddle steamer Beaver, *which served Pacific ports for more than 50 years, lies in ruins off Prospect Point in Stanley Park after running aground on July 26, 1888. Contemporary accounts hint that its crew had been celebrating before its last trip.*

after taking his astronomical readings, Fraser realized that he had not found the Columbia. He went back to the East.

David Thompson did find a route to the Columbia through the Kootenays in southeastern B.C., but he took so long to get from Lake Windermere that by the time he reached the Columbia, in July 1811, he found the Americans of John Jacob Astor's Pacific Fur Company already there, building their trading post called Fort Astoria.

Despite the squabbles between the U.S. and Britain over land around the mouth of the Columbia, the fur trade of New Caledonia prospered. The North West Company, which merged with the Hudson's Bay Company in 1821, opened new trading posts — optimistically called forts — on the rivers, lakes and trails of the Interior.

Although the Americans had sold their post on the Columbia to the Canadian company, political uncertainty encouraged the Hudson's Bay Company to seek a post farther north, with access to the Pacific and on land that had never been claimed by the increasingly aggressive American administration in Washington.

Fort Langley was built in 1827, 32 kilometres up the Fraser. It soon became a new kind of trading post: a farm and salmon-processing plant as well as warehouse and strongpoint. Vegetables, grain and fish products were shipped first to other company posts and then to other countries. A Hudson's Bay Company steamship, the *Beaver*, sailed from a Thames shipyard and around the Horn to the Columbia in 1836 and began a coastal service, picking up furs and delivering supplies.

In 1842 Hudson's Bay Company chief factor James Douglas sailed up from the Columbia and picked a site at the tip of Vancouver Island for another company post. Construction began in the spring of 1843 with the help of the Songhees people, who were paid in blankets. The new post, protected by a two-storey bastion with a nine-pounder gun, became Fort Victoria. Soon the fields around Fort Victoria were being farmed. Dairy cows were imported from the U.S., and grain and vegetables were produced to feed Fort Victoria's population and for sale to Russian fur traders on the northern coast.

As Fort Victoria was being built, the first large wave of settlers came into the Oregon Territory, and the campaign in the U.S. to control the Northwest up to 54 degrees 40 minutes north — the border with Russia — gained speed. On June 15, 1846, Britain and the United States split their differences over the border and signed the Treaty of Washington. It established the 49th parallel as the border; Britain gave up its claim to what is now Washington state and part of Oregon, and the U.S. gave up the northern border of 54/40.

Although it still had rights to trapping and trade below the new border, the Hudson's Bay Company decided to transfer its operations to Fort Victoria. In the spring of 1849, James Douglas

James Douglas was born in British Guiana in 1803, the son of a Scotsman and a Creole woman. He was educated in Scotland and joined the North West Company in 1819. Douglas served as a fur trader, joined the Hudson's Bay Company in the merger of 1821 and in 1828 married Amelia Connolly, the 16-year-old daughter of Chief Factor Connolly and a native woman. Douglas was intelligent, forceful and daring, and quickly rose to the rank of chief factor at Fort Vancouver in what is now Oregon. He built Fort Victoria in 1843 and ran the Hudson's Bay Company fiefdom from there. He became governor of Vancouver Island in 1851 and of British Columbia in 1858. Douglas retired in 1864 and died in 1877.

When the gold ran out on the Fraser River, prospectors and miners began searching closer to Vancouver. Here, photographed in 1888, are men working the Seymour Creek mine on what we now call the North Shore. The mine's capacity is listed in the Little Brown Book, a handbook for investors written by Vancouver's mayor, David Oppenheimer. The shaft, he tells readers, is from 30 feet to 40 feet deep and the ore produced at 25 feet is $8 of gold and $10 of silver to the ton.

transported his wife and daughters there and took charge of the company on Vancouver Island and in the Interior.

Douglas' wife, Amelia, was the daughter of a company fur trader and his Cree wife. She was typical of the many women of full- or half-Native blood who lived with or were married to the Scots, Orkney, Shetland and English men who worked for the company. Their daughters, educated and often brought up like English misses, married the single young men who came to the Island to farm or help run the company.

As Douglas was moving in, the Colonial Office in Westminster made Vancouver Island a Crown colony and leased it to the Hudson's Bay Company for 10 years. One of Douglas' duties, it was ordered, was to encourage settlement by men and women of English stock. This, the Colonial Office believed, was the only peaceful way to keep the pushy Americans out. Young Englishmen were encouraged to go to the Island to farm and the first, a Captain Grant, arrived in 1849. Sawmills started working to produce lumber for homes and farms, and for export to Hawaii and San Francisco. Coal mines were dug at Fort Rupert on the

Prospector Panning for Gold, Cariboo, *a painting by William Hind. He was a young British artist who came with the Overlanders in 1862 and stayed to paint before returning to Britain. The first artists who recorded life and scenery on the Pacific coast were members of the Spanish and British expeditions. Eighty years later other artists, both amateur and professional, came to paint and sketch, awed by the majesty of the mountains and fascinated by the seemingly strange life of the Native people. Then engravers and photographers took over the task of portraying British Columbia to the world.*

northern tip of the Island in 1849 and at Nanaimo in 1852. A school for girls was opened in 1849.

First Nations were the losers as farms, mills and mines were built, and they were gradually forced onto the unwanted sections of land. Douglas signed 11 land-use treaties that paid the bands cash or goods and gave them rights to hunt and fish. But the treaties left most of the land open to exploitation by the Hudson's Bay Company and settlers. Since Native people and Europeans had very different perceptions of ownership and the role of land and wildlife, the way was open for the disagreements and suspicions that were to afflict relations between them for more than 150 years.

In 1850 the first colonial governor arrived: Richard Blanshard stepped off a Royal Navy ship on March 9. No home was ready for him, and he had no salary or official funds. Seven months later he wrote his resignation letter to the Colonial Office, but he had to wait 10 months before a ship brought him a letter saying that he was relieved of his office. Douglas, in effect the real governor all along, took over officially and resigned from the Hudson's Bay Company. Blanshard had spent most of his waiting time writing letters complaining that Douglas was doing little to encourage settlement; by 1854 there were only 250 people living in the farms around Victoria.

Matthew Baillie Begbie was a 39-year-old barrister when he left England for B.C. He personified law and order in the new colony, rode on circuit like British judges and held trials when and where they were needed. Not a wisp of scandal soiled his reputation for fairness and integrity. In his first 13 years as a judge he hanged 27 men; 22 were Native. In 1884, he did his best to thwart Ottawa's ban on Native potlatch ceremonies...

Then, on Sunday, April 25, 1858, the people of Victoria came out of church to find the paddle steamer *Commodore* had just docked from San Francisco with 450 miners eager to start looking for gold.

Men had been mining underground gold for centuries, but it was a job for skilled workers and heavy equipment. Placer (free) gold, however, found in streams and near the surface, could be mined by almost anyone. In 1848 some free gold was found in Sutter's Creek in California. All was set for the first gold rush. The new telegraph and the new urban newspapers spread the news, and the new steamships were ready to carry prospectors, miners and their helpers, suppliers and entertainers to the gold.

In 1851 free gold was found by First Nations people in the Queen Charlotte Islands. Governor Douglas kept the news secret and persuaded the Colonial Office in London to give him control of the Charlottes — an invasion by the aggressive, gold- and land-hungry Americans was to be avoided at all costs.

The gold in the Charlottes fizzled out, but in 1856 Fort Victoria learned that Native people, using spoons and pieces of pottery, were scooping gold from rivers in the Interior. Douglas unilaterally extended his rule from Vancouver Island and the Charlottes to the mainland and announced regulations to govern the movement of men and supplies. This gave him some control over, and information about, the miners he expected from below the border. By the spring of 1858, the Native people in the Interior had found about 23 kilograms of gold and traded it to the Hudson's Bay Company. The nearest mint was in San Francisco, and so a company ship, the *Otter*, took the gold there.

It was not a wise decision. The news about the gold find was out, and the rush began. Soldiers left United States Army posts in northwest Washington; ship crews deserted; shopkeepers and banks lost staff. Some Americans came overland to the Fraser Valley around Lytton, Yale and Hope, where the first substantial finds were made. But most came to Victoria from California by ship; the *Commodore's* arrival on April 25 was just the first.

During April, May, June and July, about 16,000 people left California for Fort Victoria and the Fraser. Among them was a large contingent of black people who were fleeing racial restrictions in California. Other prospectors came from Hawaii, South America, eastern Canada, Europe and the United States. There are no exact figures, but one estimate is that about 30,000 people reached the Fraser River in 1858. Victoria was transformed from a small settlement around the fort into a tent and shack town devoted to housing and supplying the miners.

... and feasts by ruling against the Indian Act amendments in his courts; then the legislation was rewritten so that he was powerless. Begbie died in Victoria in 1894.

After a few days' stay in Victoria, the newcomers crossed Georgia Strait in any kind of boat or ship they could find to reach the settlements and goldfields. Over the next few years, as the Fraser Canyon gold finds grew smaller, the men moved eastward to the Similkameen and the Thompson Rivers and then north to the Cariboo and Barkerville. One 30-metre claim there is said to have produced about three kilograms of gold in one day, worth about $1,600 (price today: about $45,000).

The arrival of massive numbers of Americans onto land claimed and controlled by Britain made Westminster listen to Douglas' warnings. On August 2, 1858, the bill changing New Caledonia into the colony of British Columbia won royal assent in London. The Colonial Office had recruited a minibureaucracy to manage the new colony, and during the summer of 1858, Matthew Baillie Begbie, Chartres Brew and Colonel Richard Moody arrived in Victoria.

Begbie, 6 foot-4 inches tall, with a massive black beard, was appointed judge of the colony and soon started taking English-style justice to the settlements and goldfields. He worked with Brew, the inspector of police and chief gold commissioner, another man of power and integrity, who organized a system of constables, magistrates and courts that gave the goldfields and first settlements a simple but vigorous and sensible justice system.

Moody came to the new colony in command of a detachment of Royal Engineers whose task was to survey the land, lay out sites for cities and build trails or roads. But they were also soldiers; the

Lieutenant Colonel Richard Moody, 45 years old, came to B.C. from a command in Malta. Earlier he had been governor of the Falkland Islands. In B.C. he held three posts: commander of the B.C. Detachment of the Royal Engineers, lieutenant governor, and chief commissioner of lands and works. His men helped police the goldfields, laid out New Westminster as the capital, built roads and did surveying from their camp named Sapperton for the popular name for British army engineers, sappers. In 1863 the Royal Engineers detachment was disbanded and many of the men settled in B.C., but Moody, by now a wealthy landowner, went back to England. He died in 1887.

dust raised by the flood of Americans coming to seek gold was not the only ominous cloud in the sky over the border. In 1859 the United States Army — soon to be engaged in a civil war that would cost a million lives — crushed the indigenous people in the Washington Territory to make room for new settlers. A body of trained soldiers, even a small one like the Royal Engineers, was useful to have in the new colony at such a time.

The place of First Nations in the new British Columbia did not change as traumatically as did that of the aboriginal people south of the border. There was fighting between locals and Europeans in B.C. in the fur-trading days, but the incidents were limited and isolated. The easygoing relationship between the traders and the First Nations was based on mutual benefit and the shared hardships of life in the forests and on riverbanks. That changed as fur traders were replaced by gold miners and settlers. Now the Native people were rivals for gold and land, not allies. The miners and settlers were not employees of firms with policies about relations with Native people but entrepreneurs, out for all they could get and willing to kill for it. And the generally moderating influence of First Nations women as wives, concubines and helpers to the fur traders was lost as increasingly they were kidnapped, abused and otherwise mistreated.

This was the time, too, of the Pig War — a dispute between Britain and a cocky American administration, first over a slaughtered pig and then about control of the San Juan Islands on the border between Vancouver Island and the mainland. Governor Douglas, happy to have the Royal Navy's Pacific Squadron at Esquimalt and the Royal Engineers at hand, and buoyed by a ferment of patriotism in the people of Victoria, wanted action. But the navy advised caution, and the dispute was settled by the German emperor 13 years later — in favour of the Americans.

Gold had roused the colony. Missionaries and teachers arrived to care for the spirit and mind. Settlers began to farm around Victoria and then on Saltspring Island and in the Cowichan Valley. Some settlers started farms on the banks of the Fraser River

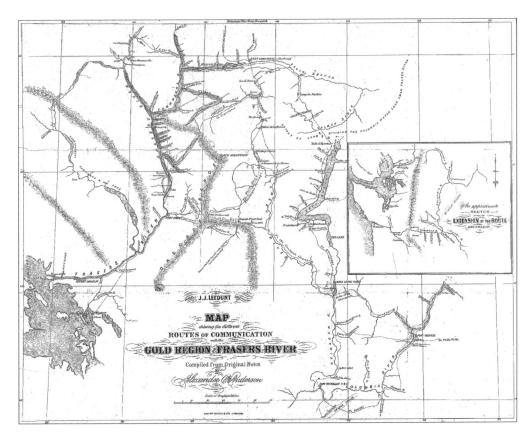

served by river steamers. Others slowly moved into the land to the south, to the areas we now call Ladner, Surrey and White Rock. In the Okanagan, along the old fur trail, cattle ranching and orchard development began. Other ranches were built in the Thompson and Nicola Valleys. The first sawmill had opened near Victoria in the late 1840s. In 1858 the first mill on the mainland was built at Yale to prepare lumber for the goldfields and settlements.

Most of the settlers picked areas already inhabited by First Nations; both groups needed settlement sites, water and easy communication. This forced First Nations off the land they used for fishing, hunting and trapping. As large parcels were granted to ranchers, Native families were left with small acreages they were

An error-filled map published in 1858 in San Francisco for would-be gold miners.

The black community of Victoria wanted to thank Governor Douglas for his welcome when they fled from racial prejudice in the United States. In 1860, when the dispute with the U.S. over control of the San Juan Islands was at its height, the black community formed the Victoria Pioneer Rifle Company, popularly called the African Rifles. Members drilled and paraded in brightly coloured uniforms sent from England, but they never left Victoria.

given in "compensation." European churches also moved in, bringing new religion, language and culture.

By the early 1860s, the first mills had started work on the north and south shores of Burrard Inlet. Most of the lumber exported went to Asia, Latin America, Australia and New Zealand; high tariffs and competitive pricing effectively closed the United States market. But at the end of the 1860s, gold still made up 75 percent of the colony's exports by value. Lumber and furs each made up 10 percent, and coal, discovered in 1849 at Fort Rupert on the northern tip of Vancouver Island and then extensively mined at Nanaimo in the next few years, made up 5 percent.

Links with the outside world grew stronger. Victoria's harbour was the centre of a network of shipping routes that ran across to the Fraser River and south to San Francisco, with connections there to the rest of the United States and the world. In 1865 the telegraph came up from San Francisco to New Westminster, and communication with London took hours rather than weeks.

The mother of the first white baby born on the mainland, Catherine Schubert came to B.C. with the Overlanders in 1862. She later told her family that while she was on the raft coming down the Thompson, she wanted to get to a settlement before her labour started so that she would have another woman to help her. She succeeded — within a few hours of reaching Kamloops, she gave birth to a daughter, with a Native woman there to help her. European women were few and far between on the mainland when Catherine Schubert gave birth. A good guess would be that there were about 1,800 European women in what we now know as B.C., most of them on Vancouver Island. The number of men: 5,000.

The flow of settlers now came overland. In the late summer of 1862, a group of 160 men, women and children left Fort Garry (now Winnipeg) in wagons on their way overland to the Cariboo goldfields. They ran out of food by the time they reached the Thompson River and, with winter coming, they had to make the last part of the journey on river rafts. They reached Kamloops in late October. A few hours later one of the party, Catherine Schubert, who had brought three children with her, gave birth to a daughter she called Rose, the first white child born on the mainland. Also in the party was an English Pre-Raphaelite artist, William Hind, who spent the next seven years painting gold miners and settlements and Victoria.

But settlement and industry grew too slowly and the shallow-rooted economic bloom generated by the gold rush began to wither. New political arrangements were necessary. Governor Douglas was getting old and new leaders were needed. Three stood out in the next few years: Dr. John Helmcken, Amor de Cosmos and John Robson.

Amor de Cosmos was born in
Nova Scotia and went to the
California gold mines to work
as a photographer. Some parts
of his life are a mystery, but
he told friends he had
changed his name from
William Smith to "lover of
the universe" to reflect his love
of mankind; his enemies said
he had to change his name
and leave California in a
hurry. Soon after he arrived
in Victoria with the gold
miners, de Cosmos started the
British Colonist *newspaper*
on a second-hand press and
used it to belabour Governor
James Douglas. De Cosmos
wanted responsible
government and fought for...

Helmcken, born in 1824, was trained in London as a doctor and had practised in other colonies before he arrived at Esquimalt in March 1850. He married one of Douglas' daughters and became Speaker of Vancouver Island's Legislative Assembly in 1856. In 1870 he was one of B.C.'s three delegates sent to Ottawa to settle the terms of Confederation.

Amor de Cosmos was born William Smith in Nova Scotia in 1825 and travelled to Victoria with gold miners from California in 1858. He stayed close to the fort, however, and started the *British Colonist* newspaper. De Cosmos entered politics and became premier in Victoria, later also serving as an MP in Ottawa. He spent his last years wandering through the streets of Victoria, a lonely and bewildered man.

Another newspaper, New Westminster's *British Columbian*, was started in 1861 by John Robson. Born in 1824 in Ontario, he came to British Columbia in 1859. After the capital of B.C. was moved to Victoria from New Westminster in 1868, he followed in 1869 to be the editor of de Cosmos' *British Colonist*. Robson fought for responsible and representative government and for Confederation, and served on the Legislative Council and in the Legislature. He left newspapers and politics in 1875 to become paymaster for the surveyors laying out the Canadian Pacific Railway. In 1882 he was again a member of the Legislature, serving as minister of finance and agriculture, and then as premier.

Slowly the parts of the puzzle were put, or pushed, into place. Douglas retired in 1864 and the new governor from England, Frederick Seymour, pressed for the merger of the two debt-ridden colonies of Vancouver Island and British Columbia. It came on August 2, 1866, but did little to solve the economic crisis.

British Columbians had three choices: 1) stay a British colony and hope for more help but maintain less control, 2) join the United States or 3) join the rest of Canada.

The first option was unattractive, for the Colonial Office showed little sympathy for the desires and needs of an insignificant colony halfway around the world. The second seemed attractive,

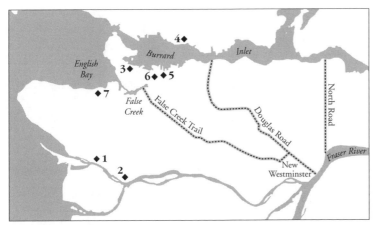

... democracy in the Island's Legislative Assembly and on the B.C. Legislative Council. He also fought for union with Canada and organized the Confederation League, which met at Yale in September 1868. But his eccentricity and sarcastic speech alienated many, and less controversial men were chosen to negotiate the terms of Confederation in Ottawa in 1870. De Cosmos was still popular with voters, however, and was later elected a federal MP and then premier. While in Ottawa, he started a provincial fad: he called for B.C. to separate from Canada.

for the U.S. Civil War was over, and prosperity was moving swiftly across the plains to the Pacific. Petitions advocating joining the United States circulated in Victoria, where most of the businesses had been started by Americans; the United States consul in Victoria sent Washington encouraging dispatches. The third option did not make much sense; British Columbia was separated from Canada by thousands of kilometres of trackless wilderness.

Then, in March 1867, the U.S. bought Alaska from Russia for $7.2 million. Was B.C. trapped between two massive tracts of U.S. territory? Three months later the provinces in the east joined in a confederation and started to extend control over the land between Ontario and British Columbia. Would Canada be a better saviour now?

De Cosmos formed the Confederation League in 1868, and Robson joined him. In 1869 Governor Seymour, weakened by years of relentless drinking, died from dysentery. The new governor, Anthony Musgrave, arrived from Newfoundland with Colonial Office orders to speed the union with Canada. In the bars and homes of Victoria, New Westminster and the other tiny settlements, the arguments were fierce and long. The Legislative Council in Victoria, spurred on by Musgrave and after seemingly endless debate, agreed to terms proposed by the governor.

Musgrave picked three delegates to go to Ottawa to propose

THIS PAGE:
First settlements on
Burrard Inlet:
1. Musqueam village
2. Great Fraser Midden
First European settlements,
1860s:
3. John Morton's shack near
present Marine Building
4. Pioneer Mills, later Moody's
5. Stamp's Mill
6. Gassy Jack's saloon
7. Jerry Rogers' logging camp
on Jerry's Cove, now Jericho

Anthony Musgrave was the governor of Newfoundland when the British Colonial Office appointed him to succeed Governor Seymour in B.C. He was a friend of Sir John A. Macdonald and was known as a supporter of B.C.'s joining Canada. An affable, jolly man, Musgrave was told to make certain that the B.C. Legislative Council voted in favour of Confederation; he quickly realized that money and a railway link were the keys. Musgrave told Ottawa and London that cash grants, pensions for administrators who would lose their jobs and a railway would do the trick. Ottawa, pressed by London, accepted his advice.

the terms of joining Confederation. On May 14, 1870, Helmcken, Lands Commissioner John Trutch (who took his wife, Amelia) and Dr. Robert Carrall from the Cariboo sailed from Victoria to San Francisco on the wooden paddle steamer *Active*. After three days' shopping and visiting, they crossed San Francisco Bay to Oakland, where they got on a Central Pacific train. This was to take them to Promontory, Utah, where the last spike of the U.S. transcontinental railway had been driven a year before. There they would change to the Union Pacific, which ran along the old Oregon Trail to Omaha and Nebraska and on to Detroit, where they would board a Canadian train to take them to Ottawa.

On the long journey there was much to talk about: what was Henry Seelye, one of the editors of the Victoria *Daily Colonist*, up to? He had travelled with the delegates from Victoria to

San Francisco but had left for Ottawa on an earlier train. The delegates feared he would try to convince Ottawa that it should make the establishment of responsible and representative government one condition of joining Canada. They were also afraid that he would telegraph the results of his talks back to Victoria.

Helmcken wanted more open government, but for Carrall and Trutch, other things mattered much more: getting money to pay British Columbia's debts; substantial per capita grants; guaranteed pensions for civil servants.

All three delegates wanted union with Canada and some kind of overland link with central Canada. A railway, like the one that was taking them east, would be nice, but Carrall and Trutch would settle for a wagon road. Helmcken wanted the railway.

Some idea of his care for patients — and of Victorian surgery — comes from artist-author Emily Carr: "Dr. Helmcken attended to all our ailments ... he even told us what to do when the cat ... ... had fits. You began to get better the moment you heard him coming up the stairs ..."

This extract is part of an agenda paper contributed by the Mowachaht-Nuchatlaht First Nations, who live on the west coast of Vancouver Island, to a book published by the Royal British Columbia Museum, Nuu-chah-nulth Voices, Histories, Objects and Journeys. *Our history has always been told by the European explorers and traders, they complained. Now it's our turn.*

For most people, Yuquot is a small village on the wind-swept west coast of Vancouver Island; for the Mowachaht-Nuchatlaht people, however, Yuquot is the centre of the world, and the winds bring food and visitors to their doors.

Yuquot,
the Centre of the World

Yuquot. It is the centre of the world. The name of our village, meaning "where the wind blows from all directions," acknowledges the central nature of the place given to us by the Creator. During the winter when the powerful winds sweep unhindered from the southwest across the open ocean, we wonder why some of the rocks on the beach don't blow away. In the spring, it arrives from the west with news of the sea, of the arrival of the herring and whales. In the summer, the wind comes from the southeast, following the shores of Vancouver Island and warming the land. This is the breeze that guided men like Cook, Bodega y Quadra, Malaspina and Meares who, with their ships, visited our harbour over two hundred years ago. In the fall, the wind brings the first storms and heavy rains, beckoning the salmon to return to their river homes, signaling to our people the last great harvest of the year. Last, the wind comes from the north, twisting overland across the forest and mountains. This wind is filled with the scent and spirit of the cedar, fir and yew, of the mountains, inlets, streams, rivers and lakes that feed the richness of our territory.

Yuquot also is at the centre for gathering the resources which have nourished us through countless generations. It is ideally located between the land and the sea, between the outside and the inside, between the abundance and energy of the ocean and the majesty and richness of the forest and inlets. It is a place of power and change. We look to the outside, to the open Pacific, for the whales, sea lions and seals, to the fishing banks for halibut, cod and salmon, and to the rocky shorelines for mussels and barnacles. To the inside are the sheltered waters, providing us with clams, oysters and herring, and the forests which sustain us with cedar, alder, berries, plants, deer, elk and much more. Further inside, up the inlets, are the rivers that once were rich with spawning salmon, and trails that led up through the mountains across Vancouver Island to our neighbours with whom we have always traded.

To outsiders, Yuquot appears to be at the edge of the world. For us, it is the centre of the world. It is a place of unsurpassed beauty and natural wonders we wish all to witness. A place where one can share a beach with whales who come to rub in the surf, where one can feel the power of the great winds, experience Nature's harmonies, and travel back in time to ponder people and events that once were.

Yuquot is also the centre of our history, a place of many stories, some of which we will share with you. Our history extends far back, to the very beginnings of time. One of our stories tells of the time when the Great Creator made the first woman in the wilderness at Yuquot. She, in turn, produced "Snot-Boy," who eventually grew to become the first man of our nation. Together, they produced the offspring of whom we are the direct descendants. Other stories document the early history of Yuquot, the origins of the many powerful tribes who once inhabited our territory, the wars and conflicts which took place, and the experiences of Yahlua, the father of the first Chief Maquinna. Some of our most important history lessons document the origins and development of the whaling power, and how the Whalers' Washing House came to be the source of that power. All of our history demonstrates the interconnectedness of life, and illustrates the deep spiritual bonds we have with our environment as a result of the experiences, adventures and keen observations of our ancestors.

Archaeologists undertaking excavations at Yuquot unearthed the remains of some of the foods our ancestors ate, tools they used, and other items of house and hearth. From these few clues, they developed theories about our history and the development of our culture, and say they have proof we have lived at Yuquot for over 4,300 years. We suspect that further research will prove we have been there much longer, and will reveal much more information about our way of life.

TWO

1871 TO 1900

Growing Up and Filling Out

B.C. society in the 19th century was dominated by the family. Individuals, particularly women, who had no family support were virtual outsiders. Only within the family could women achieve any power or status. Here the Gorden family of Bella Coola, three generations strong and with mother and grandmother in the centre, poses for the prized group portrait. At a discreet distance to the back are the hired hands, family members of a kind. Large families for the middle class meant care in old age. For the poor they meant more income as the children were sent out to work.

John Helmcken returned to Victoria on July 18, 1870, and told Governor Musgrave about the delegates' success in Ottawa. The other delegates, Carrall and Trutch, had followed what was to be a familiar pattern for British Columbia politicians: they added some personal visiting to the end of their official trip east. Mr. and Mrs. Trutch went to England and Carrall went back to his home in Ontario. Helmcken found he could tell Musgrave little new: Seelye had been sending dispatches from Ottawa to the *Colonist* as well as lobbying for more democratic government, and official dispatches had kept Musgrave informed about the talks.

British Columbia was promised what it had sought. London was eager to be rid of a colony nearly 10,000 kilometres away and made certain that the new dominion made the new province welcome. True, the per capita grants were not as generous as expected, but that loss was matched by Ottawa's generosity in promising construction of a railway to the coast within years and in the guarantees of provincial pensions.

British Columbia had asked for a wagon road and then a railway. Now the railway was to be started at both ends, like the

American transcontinental, so that the new province would get benefits at the beginning. And Seelye's work had made John Robson, Amor de Cosmos and the other advocates of political freedom happy. Ottawa had made it clear that British Columbia was to start its life as a province of Canada with responsible government and a fully elected legislature.

The whinging suspicion of Ottawa, so much a part of political life for the next 150 years, was there at the start. Many Victorians were not so easily pleased. You were tricked, Helmcken was told by people he met in the street. The railway will never be built. Canadians are too stingy. And why won't Victoria be the terminus? But when the Legislative Council met on January 5, 1871, it approved the terms of union unanimously. In another foreshadowing, none of the delegates received any recognition or thanks from their fellow British Columbians. Carrall was made a senator by Ottawa, however, and Trutch was feted in the capital and made the province's first lieutenant governor. Helmcken went back to work as a doctor.

The new province's society was typically colonial — First

Government Street, Victoria, in the 1860s. Flimsy wooden buildings, each built to its owner's taste, enclose a dusty street. When the rain turns the dust into mud, there's the boardwalk. A horse-drawn cart and a water wagon take their time, for there are few reasons to hurry.

The church was the social centre of the European community. Here, it's 1908 and a newly wedded couple is coming out of Christ Church in Vancouver. For the crowd outside, many of whom have come on bicycle, now's the chance to congratulate the couple and enjoy the occasion.

Nations were in the majority, Europeans a minority and women a small proportion of those. About 30 percent of the Europeans who lived on the tip of Vancouver Island and in New Westminster were female, and women made up about 10 percent of the settlers living in the Interior. Their style of living with their husbands (for there were virtually no unmarried females over 25) was determined by wealth and social status. In the cities of Victoria and, to a lesser extent, New Westminster, the middle class tried to recreate the life they had left behind, or that their parents had told them about. Respectability and propriety were paramount. Families were relatively large because any kind of contraception was secret and regarded as immoral. As in the industrial society they had left, middle-class women performed practically no work outside the home. Bearing and nurturing children, running the home, supporting their husbands and appearing decorative to bolster their husbands' social position were their duties.

Women whose husbands had less money led less restricted but harder lives. Many played active roles in farming and ranching and for them, child-bearing appeared just an added task. Although childbed was becoming less dangerous, the chance of losing a baby in the first years was still high. Children's diseases, the low immunity of children to all kinds of disease and the sorry state of medical science meant parents lived in fear until their offspring reached 15 years or so. Amelia Douglas, the governor's wife, gave birth to 13 children, but only five survived her.

Medicine had progressed slowly and although surgery, antiseptics and simple drugs were available by this time, diagnosis was difficult, medical information scanty and training very poor. Dr. Helmcken told how he was reluctant to use carbolic acid as an antiseptic for Governor Musgrave when he broke his ankle and blamed the governor's permanent lameness on another doctor who used it profusely. Outside the cities, medical help was virtually nonexistent. Instead, recipes and cures were handed down from mother to daughter.

By the mid-1870s, the largest city, Victoria, saved from economic ruin when the capital was moved from New Westminster in 1868, had shed all traces of the late 1850s and its role as the base for thousands of miners and prospectors. Many of the Americans who had come in the gold rush days had gone back to the United States to enjoy the prosperity that followed the end of the Civil War and construction of the railroads in the West. There were still about 5,000 people living in the city. Now the shacks had gone and Victoria's buildings were built of stone and brick; the streets were paved, and lit by gas.

Social life for the city's elite was staid and predictable. The presence of the Royal Navy's Pacific Squadron provided genteel

*D*iseases, such as measles, tuberculosis, smallpox, influenza, venereal diseases and alcoholism were introduced to B.C. by outsiders. Most Europeans were immune to smallpox, the most deadly of the illnesses, by exposure or vaccination, by the early 19th century. Natives were unprotected. A smallpox epidemic in northern B.C. in 1780 nearly decimated the Tlingit and Haida communities, killing an estimated 60,000 people. In Fort Simpson in 1836, about one-third of the Tsimshian population was destroyed. In 1860, in Victoria and among other communities along the coast, another 20,000 Natives died.

Two views of spiritual life.
ABOVE: First Nations people at
a potlatch ceremony.

competition for the company of young women at the balls and parties that filled the social season. The Theatre Royal provided a home for touring companies and local amateurs, and the Philharmonic Society offered concerts and recitals for music lovers. Tennis courts were necessities for the wealthy, encouraged by Chief Justice Begbie, who gave the best tennis parties.

A school system with central control had been planned under Governor Douglas, but a shortage of money hampered progress. After Confederation, John Jessop was appointed school superintendent, and in 1872 he introduced legislation for a school system with free universal education that has been the measure ever since. A Central High School was opened in 1877. Jessop even set his sights on a university. Some university degrees were awarded through arrangements with McGill in Montreal in the late 19th century, but the University of B.C. did not open until 1915.

First Nations people dressed in European styles in front of a Christian church in Squamish, 1890.

Anglican, Roman Catholic and Methodist ministers had followed the first settlers to Vancouver Island. They had two objectives: to provide schools and pastoral services to the Hudson's Bay Company officers, men and the settlers, and to convert the Native people to Christianity. First in the Victoria area was Father Modeste Demers, named bishop of Vancouver Island in 1847. An Anglican, Reverend Robert Staines, arrived two years later with his wife to run a boarding school and give Anglican services. In 1858 four Sisters of St. Anne came from Quebec to set up Roman Catholic schools in Victoria and New Westminster. By the 1860s, a Methodist minister was paddling a canoe up the Fraser River to preach to the gold miners. A synagogue was soon built in Victoria. As settlers opened up the Lower Mainland and the Interior, the churches moved with them.

The churches preached a social gospel, too. In 1862 and 1863 the Anglicans, realizing that a society with so few women lacked stability, brought two bride ships to Victoria. Records are scanty, but it's difficult to call the experiment successful. Some women married settlers, but others joined the local prostitutes. In 1862 William Duncan, an Anglican appalled by the effects of European society on the Native people living north of what is now Prince Rupert, persuaded them to move to a Utopia-like community he created at a Tsimshian village called Metlakatla.

The churches were the chief proponents of a ban on potlatches introduced as amendments to Ottawa's Indian Act in 1884. British Columbia had no legislation to govern or protect First Nations but Ottawa assumed responsibility for them as part of the Confederation agreement.

Missionaries, priests and congregations disregarded the spiritual side of potlatches and regarded them as extravagant, wasteful, drunken and cruel ceremonies that distracted First Nations people. Christianity, hard work and thrift should be the rule. The message was sent to Ottawa and potlatches were banned. Some bands, especially in the more remote parts of the coast, defied Ottawa's "Indian agents" for many years. In 1922 the Kwakiutl held a massive potlatch at Alert Bay and invited other bands. It was raided by police and the chiefs were told they could go free if they gave up their regalia. Most agreed and some of the masks, artwork, figures and other treasures went to the National Museum in Ottawa, with collectors skimming off some pieces. (Much of the material was returned to the First Nations in 1980.)

*O*nce settlers and miners arrived, Native culture was under attack. Soon traditional costume vanished and European clothes became the norm. Chiefs who cooperated were given militia-style uniforms. The nudity or seminudity of some Natives disturbed the overclothed settlers and missionaries; they soon had the women in long skirts and sweaters and men in jackets and trousers. Traditional dress was reserved for private ceremonies.

The worst blow came in 1884 when the Indian Act was amended to ban the gift-giving and feasting of the coastal bands' potlatch. To the Europeans, these ceremonies were occasions for drunkenness, debauchery and paganism. To First Nations, they were an integral part of the spiritual life that bonded them to the land, the creatures of the sea and forests, and to each other. Some bands defied the ban and held potlatch ceremonies in secret. The ban was lifted in 1951.

As more settlers arrived, pressures on the traditional life of the First Nations increased. Many Europeans were convinced that they had a mission to bring their kind of civilization to the aboriginals. What they saw of the Native people who lived around the cities and settlements confirmed their prejudices: drunkenness, prostitution and disease had made some Native people pathetic creatures whose plight wrung the hearts of missionaries and well-intentioned matrons.

These were the outward and visible signs of the inward and spiritual corruption that had started at the beginning of the century. Unfortunately, the evangelical spirit, if not the beliefs, of many of the settlers and new town dwellers encouraged the work of missionaries who tried to convert the First Nations to Christianity and a foreign — and for them, destructive — way of living.

Under Governor Douglas, the old fur trader, Native people had received sympathetic treatment. He tried to protect their villages, fishing places, hunting sites and fields against settlers, because he

A group of Chinese workers on the CPR. They were paid much less than Europeans but did the most dangerous and menial tasks and lived in the worst camps. When the railway was finished, they settled in cities and villages, found other work and started new communities. The CPR would not have been built without them.

NORTH PACIFIC LUMBER Co's MILL

On the shores of Vancouver Island, Burrard Inlet and the rivers and lakes in the Interior, mills like this converted logs cut nearby into construction lumber and planks. This is the North Pacific Lumber Company mill in Barnet, just west of Port Moody.

believed they and Europeans could prosper together. But Douglas retired in 1864, and Joseph Trutch took over Indian Affairs as part of his job as commissioner of works. The protective shield around Native settlements was broken, and the whittling away of Native lands and customs gathered speed.

First Nations leaders expected improvement when British Columbia joined Canada, for relationships with them were more sympathetically handled in other provinces. First Nations people made up about 70 percent of the province's population at this time, but they were not involved in any political decisions. Despite, or perhaps because of, the appointment of federal Indian Affairs officers, the tensions between Native people and settlers grew, chiefly over land and Native women. The building of the Canadian Pacific railway in the province in the early 1880s made the situation worse. Native people received no compensation for the vast tracts of land given to the CPR, and the construction camps became sinks of degradation for many Native men and women.

Native people joined Europeans in distrusting the Chinese, however. During the first 10 years of Confederation, the number of Chinese in the province doubled, and by 1881 there were around 4,000. Chinese immigrants had first arrived in Victoria as part of the flood into the colony from the United States in 1858. Some followed the miners up the Fraser; others stayed to work as servants and laundrymen in Victoria, where they were joined by hundreds sailing directly from Hong Kong. Their dress, apparent reluctance to join in European society and the preference of some for opium rather than alcohol made them victims of abuse and prejudice. Following the example of the builders of the U.S. transcontinental railroad, contractor Andrew Onderdonk — short of labourers for the British Columbia section of the Canadian Pacific railway — brought in 2,000 mainland Chinese in May 1881. By the time the line was finished in November 1885, more than two-thirds of the 13,000 men working on the railway were Chinese. When work ended, most drifted back to the coast and became a constant irritant to the burghers of Victoria and Vancouver.

Settlement depended on the economy, and until work started on the railway, few new immigrants came to the province. But some small groups of men and their families started to live around the first sawmills, fish plants and mines. There were few roads and

Ethnic Groups in British Columbia

1770	First Nations: 90,000		
1871	First Nations: 26,000	British & European: 17,000	Asian: 4,300
1901	First Nations: 29,000	British & European: 127,000	Asian: 19,500
1941	First Nations: 25,000	British & European: 740,000	Asian: 42,500
1981	First Nations: 73,670	British & European: 2,400,000	Asian: 205,000
1991	First Nations: 118,731	British & European: 2,700,000	Asian: 392,000

Building a railway through the Fraser Canyon was a daunting task. Tunnels and bridges dotted the track, clinging dangerously to the rocky walls of the canyon. Heavy snowfalls often closed the track for weeks.

no amenities or comforts. For men, women and children, life consisted of a daily struggle to keep dry and warm and get some simple food inside them. Food had to come from the sea, the river, their own gardens and small fields and the forests. Hunting deer, rabbits and other game brought a change to a monotonous diet. Many clothes, tools, utensils and items of furniture were handmade, for there were few stores and usually there was no way to get to them. Social life, too, had to be handmade and it centred around the church or school or one of the larger homes.

By the early 1880s, there were about 200 people engaged in mixed farming in Langley, Delta and Richmond. About the same number tried to grow grain and raise cattle in the Okanagan and southern Interior. Lumbering, often a one-man or one-family operation, was confined to the coast where the giant logs, some nearly three metres thick, could be rolled into the water to be taken to the nearest mill. Most of the fish were caught by Native people, but canneries opened in the 1870s and attracted European communities to places where the fish could be landed, cut, cleaned, boiled and canned as quickly as possible — the Fraser, Skeena and Nass

Rivers estuaries. As the goldfields dwindled and communities such as Barkerville slowly became backwaters, other mining communities grew up in the Kootenays close to the U.S. border and smelters.

Slowly, too, small communities grew around Burrard Inlet, long recognized as a strategic centre for both military and economic purposes and yet strangely deserted. The first settlement in what is now the Vancouver area came in September 1862, when the McCleery family started farming on the north shore of the Fraser. Soon much of the land close to the river up to what is now Chilliwack had been cleared and cultivated — only to be taken back by nature in the great flood of 1893.

Three disappointed miners decided to settle in the area now known as the West End in 1862, and by the late 1870s, there were hotels, shacks and mills on the shores of the inlet and two communities called Hastings and Granville. Only 700 or so people lived there.

The Skuzzy *was the only steamboat to pass upriver through the Hells Gate rapids. The typical small sternwheeler was built by Andrew Onderdonk's engineers at Tunnel City, near Spuzzum, about 32 kilometres upriver from Yale and about 1.5 kilometres below Hells Gate.*

The crowning moment: on November 7, 1885, the track laid by Andrew Onderdonk's men meets the track from the Prairies, and the "Last Spike" is hammered home in a clearing called Craigellachie. Donald Smith (Lord Strathcona), fur trader turned financier, does the honours. Craigellachie, 45 kilometres west of Revelstoke, was named after a rock in Banffshire, Scotland: both CPR president George Stephen and Smith came from the area.

That was soon to change. In May 1880 work began at Yale, about 190 kilometres to the east, on the British Columbia section of the railway that would turn Burrard Inlet and its tiny communities into a large city. Just over five years later, on November 7, 1885, the eastward and westward tracks were joined at Craigellachie in the mountains. Soon afterward, the first train from the east arrived in Port Moody, a small village tucked away at the head of the inlet.

Port Moody was not the harbour the CPR wanted, however, for it was too shallow for ocean-going ships. Granville was more like it and, after a gift of about 2,400 hectares from the provincial government and some more from far-sighted local entrepreneurs, the CPR built tracks along the southern shore of Burrard Inlet. The boom that resulted rivalled the gold rush. Granville became the city of Vancouver on April 6, 1886, burned to the ground two months later and was rebuilt almost as quickly. The city's growth was fuelled by the arrival of the first passenger train from Montreal

After the bustle of building the CPR, Yale sleeps in the midday sun in this 1890 photograph. Like many of the communities on the railway's route, Yale for a few years was home to a horde of engineers, surveyors, sailors, tracklayers and labourers. There also were men and women working in what we now call the service industries.

on May 23, 1887, and the docking of the first passenger ship from Asia, the *Abyssinia*, three weeks later.

In short order, real-estate men and engineers had the business and residential sections laid out, roads and sewers built and street lights turned on. Banks, hotels, business blocks and shops sprang up. Boarding houses and shacks filled with the clerks and workers who would help the businessmen turn native forest into profitable asphalt jungle. Schools and an opera house followed. Nearly everyone in the city came from somewhere else and wanted all the trappings of the cities they had left behind duplicated, to make Vancouver like home.

But visitors complained that the city lacked character; the only reasons for its existence were money and the CPR. Streetcars started running on routes carefully planned to favour CPR holdings. As they passed offices and plants, the streetcars sucked so much current from the power system that lights went out and machines stopped.

It had taken Victoria more than 40 years to go from settlement to city. Vancouver did it in less than one-tenth of the time.

Andrew Onderdonk, who built the CPR from Port Moody to Eagle Pass, moved to Yale in 1880 with his wife, Delia, and their four children. From there he supervised the blasting, building and grading that took the track through the forbidding Fraser Canyon. Reserved, always smartly dressed, Onderdonk was backed by a syndicate of bankers in New York and San Francisco. By 1883 he had run out of money and went to Ottawa to get help but was refused, so he cut costs drastically by tightening the curves of the track and generally lowering standards...

The gold rush of 1858 turned British Columbia into a colony. Union with Canada in 1871 made it a province. The coming of the railway in 1885 started the transition from a backwater into a modern industrial state.

It's time, then, to go back a bit and look at how the railway was built and how it saved, and transformed, British Columbia.

Those 14 years between admission into Confederation and the driving of the "last spike" were anxious years for British Columbia's politicians and businessmen. They worried that Ottawa would renege on its promise to start the railway in two years and be finished within 10. The economy was in tatters. Gold was no longer the mainspring of the economy and the other major industries — forestry, fishing and hard-rock mining — were not yet strong enough to make up the loss. Everyone waited for the railway that would, they believed, bring settlers, goods and investment and open Canada and the eastern United States as a market for British Columbia.

Political life in B.C. at this time was as weak as the economy. The long tradition of its politicians complaining and fighting Ottawa, rather than trying to solve their problems, got its start in the first years after the colony joined Confederation.

Finding enough intelligent persons who are willing to serve in politics is a universal problem. The needs of government often outstrip the supply of competent, well-educated, sensible — and willing — people. British Columbia has never been free of this syndrome, especially so in the late 19th century. The European population numbered only about 9,000, and from this tiny group the province had to provide three senators and elect six members of Parliament and 25 members of the Legislature.

There were no political parties, just a continuum of shifting pressure groups that made it difficult for premiers to embark on any kind of program. In the first 32 years of democracy in British Columbia (1871–1903), 14 men served as premiers, about one every two years.

The businessmen, professionals and civil servants who formed the political elite of the province spent most of their time squabbling with Ottawa about the railway and about money. In spare moments, they stirred up arguments between those who lived on the mainland and those who liked life in Victoria and wanted to make certain that the long-awaited railway ended on their doorstep.

Threats to secede — a regular component of British Columbia's politics then, as now — enlivened the debate. Concerned citizens signed petitions to Queen Victoria. They joined protests to persuade the visiting governor general to meddle.

There were reasons to be worried, it's true. Sir John A. Macdonald, the generous Conservative prime minister of the Confederation negotiations, left office in 1873 under a cloud of scandal. Surveys for the railway had started, but the Liberals did not share Macdonald's transcontinental dream; their leader, Alexander Mackenzie, thought it was mad. And when the railway plans were revived in 1877, it became obvious that Ottawa favoured a route ending in an almost-deserted Burrard Inlet rather than one ending at Esquimalt, in the centre of British Columbia's most populated area.

But in September 1878, Sir John A. was re-elected to enact his so-called National Plan, with tariffs and the railway as its main thrusts. While Ottawa was still negotiating the final terms with the Canadian Pacific Railway Company, work began on the British Columbia section (the one to be built by the federal government) near Yale, in the Fraser Canyon, in May 1880. The contractor was Andrew Onderdonk, a 37-year-old American who was backed by a wealthy New York syndicate. He had lost his original bids on the various federal government contracts to build the line from Port Moody to Kamloops but, with Ottawa's connivance, had bought the contracts from lower bidders.

In addition to massive land grants and a $25 million subsidy, Ottawa had agreed to hand over to the CPR this part of the line once it was built. Onderdonk was building a railway that would be operated by someone else. His cost-cutting measures — such as building

... After the CPR took over, the company had to spend heavily to improve the track. Onderdonk later built canals, bridges and railways in the United States, Canada and Argentina.

Delia Onderdonk played a traditional role in the building of the CPR. She entertained the notables who came to inspect her husband's work and ran a hospital for the many workers injured by explosions and other accidents.

The first passenger train from Montreal to the Pacific, headed by wood-burning locomotive No. 371, reached Port Moody at noon on July 4, 1886. About 1,500 people from Vancouver Island, New Westminster and Burrard Inlet came to picnic, listen to concerts and greet the train and its passengers.

numerous tight curves and forbidding gradients — might be good for a money-conscious contractor, but they would make the running of trains through the canyon dangerous and expensive.

For the first year Onderdonk blasted away up the canyon, maiming or killing hundreds of workers as rocks fell and explosives caught fire. Since no track had been laid, he had to move construction machinery, tools and food by mule and oxen teams over the trail built by Governor Douglas 20 years before. Costs were so high that Onderdonk decided in 1882 to build his own 250-tonne river steamer, the *Skuzzy*. His plan: to sail it through Hells Gate and its 10-knot current into a relatively calmer stretch upriver. Then he would use the vessel to carry cargo and men between Boston Bar and Lytton. At first no skipper would take the *Skuzzy* through; those who tried nearly wrecked the vessel. Onderdonk took charge. He ordered ring bolts driven into the

The settlement of Granville, shown here looking west from Hastings Mill in 1886, was incorporated as the City of Vancouver on April 6 that year. It was destroyed by fire two months later. The blaze started in a clearing and quickly leaped from treetop to treetop until it surrounded the built-up area where, encouraged by a stiff breeze, it turned wooden buildings into instant bonfires. Most people escaped by running out of town or by wading into the water. No one knows how many died, though some say about 20. Rebuilding started the next morning.

canyon walls and ropes passed through them. A steam winch on board, helped by crewmen pulling on the capstan and a horde of Chinese labourers pulling perilously on shore, eventually pulled the *Skuzzy* through.

At first Onderdonk had been unable to find enough white and Native workmen — perhaps because his payscale ($1.75 a day) was less than that of American railroad contractors. Then he remembered that Chinese labourers had helped build the American transcontinental, and so he started to employ Chinese workers. They were paid only $1 a day, demanded no camps or cooks and were less troublesome when work was done than the whites or Native people.

British Columbians were horrified that Onderdonk had hired Chinese. They not only looked different, they thought and acted differently and seemed a threat to civilization as white British Columbians knew it. To keep the Chinese out, a series of anti-Chinese laws and taxes was devised, but they weren't successful; in 1882 Onderdonk brought in another 6,000 workers directly from China. Even with all this help, he had laid only about 32 kilometres

The CPR took over the coastal fleet of Canadian Pacific Navigation in 1901. A short time later the Islander, *shown here, and one of its prize passenger ships, hit an iceberg near Skagway, Alaska. One of the CP Navigation ships taken over was called the* Princess Louise, *and soon most of the CPR's coastal fleet took "Princess" names, matching its ocean fleet's Empresses.*

of track two years after he had started work, so difficult was the task of blasting and cutting a way along the side of the canyon.

Once Onderdonk's men had conquered the canyon, the going was relatively easy. By August 1885 they had gone past Kamloops and were building the line to Eagle Pass to link with the mountain section being built by the CPR. By October Onderdonk's crews reached Eagle Pass, and on the morning of November 7 the tracks were joined at a clearing in the forest called Craigellachie. The Last Spike was driven home. The workers went back to their huts and camps to celebrate and to look for new jobs. The railway directors and contractors climbed into their train, headed by a little wood-burning eight-wheeler, that took them, in a happy mood, to Port Moody and the Pacific Ocean.

The winter shut down the transcontinental line in the mountains. When the line opened in the spring, only works and freight trains came through. The first passenger train from Montreal did not arrive in Port Moody until July 4, 1886, after a journey of 139 hours, and more than 1,000 people greeted it. Fourteen kilometres to the west of the terminus, the railway's surveyors had already started to lay out the new townsite on 2,400 hectares they owned around the little settlement called Granville. They drove their first spike in the forest at what is now Victory Square, and Vancouver was soon the ultimate company town, with the CPR's hand in

almost every action, every deal. But the company did not want to stop in Vancouver. Out in the Pacific were more goods, more people. Three ocean-going ships, the *Abyssinia*, *Parthia* and *Batavia*, were chartered in 1887 to carry freight (mostly tea and silk) and passengers from Yokohama, Shanghai and Hong Kong to the new port on the Pacific. Three gleaming white liners, the *Empress of Japan*, *Empress of China* and *Empress of India* were built in British shipyards in 1891–2. Each displaced 6,000 tonnes — roughly the same size (but not shape) as a modern British Columbia ferry — and made about 16 knots.

Sternwheelers were easily built, adaptable vessels of shallow draft that could be run ashore anywhere to land passengers and cargo. They sailed the rivers and lakes, especially in southeastern B.C., and filled the gaps in the railway system.

The first of them, the *Empress of India*, docked off Victoria early on April 28, 1891. It had left Liverpool, England, in February with a select group of passengers on a round-the-world tour before picking up cargo and other passengers in India, China and Japan.

The first of the Canadian Pacific Railway's Empress liners, the Empress of India, *arrives in Vancouver from Japan on April 28, 1891, after an 11-day voyage. Most offices and homes in the city were deserted as crowds braved the rain to welcome the ship. Cornelius Van Horne, president of the CPR, and Vancouver's mayor and aldermen come to tour it and some of the aldermen were disturbed by the large amount of space allotted to steerage passengers, which they thought might encourage the Chinese.*

The *Empress* then made a record 11-day run from Yokohama. Most of the people in Victoria left jobs and homes to see the ship arrive. After a round of speeches and presentations, the liner steamed to Vancouver to dock at the CPR's Cordova wharf in the early afternoon. Now it was Vancouver's turn: crowds covered the dock and the usual stuffed shirts made speeches and forecast prosperity for all now that the wise, all-seeing CPR had seen fit to send these wonderful ships. They wondered, however, whether the holds for steerage passengers were too large and would encourage a flood of Chinese. The 100 world-tour passengers then got on a CPR train for the East and a return voyage across the Atlantic. Other passengers could stay at the new Hotel Vancouver.

The CPR had realized that passengers would need a first-rate hotel to stay in before and after they boarded trains and ships, and work had started in July 1886 at the corner of Granville and Georgia.

The new hotel would be easy to find, for on August 8, 1887, the Vancouver Electric Illumination Society (later B.C. Electric, and still later B.C. Hydro) started up its steam-powered generating

The first Hotel Vancouver was built on Granville Street on the site now occupied by the Eatons store. The hotel opened just before the first passenger train arrived, when Granville was a new street and workers had just finished clearing the forest from the docks to False Creek. No one could say that it was a beautiful building, and it had to be enlarged soon after it was built. Few shops or offices were opened to keep the hotel company, and Cordova stayed the main street until the turn of the century. The hotel's successor was built a block away, but was only half-finished when construction was stopped during the Depression.

plant at the corner of Abbott and Hastings. Three hundred street lights went on, and the oil lamps were put away in 53 Vancouver homes.

The transcontinental railway's arrival in Vancouver meant a much larger coastal shipping service was needed. More passengers and freight had to be carried to Vancouver Island and the Puget Sound area, and to the fishing and logging camps, canneries, mills and other settlements being built up the coast. The Hudson's Bay Company, which had provided coastal service for most of the century, had joined other firms in 1883 to form the Canadian Pacific Navigation Company, which took over a motley fleet of stern-

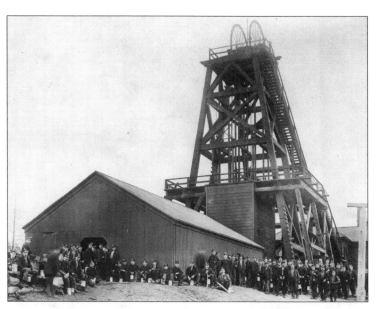

Coal mines like this one were sunk on Vancouver Island and in the Interior to feed the furnaces of shipping fleets and sawmills and factories. This photograph of workers waiting to go down the shaft at a mine near Nanaimo shows a picture of calm, but the peace was often broken by the blare of whistles and shouts as crews tried to rescue victims of underground explosions. B.C.'s early coal mines had more than a fair share of disasters.

wheelers and steamers of all sizes. Now, to handle the extra traffic from the CPR and Great Northern railways, the company ordered the *Premier*, a 15-knot steamer with room for 300 passengers, from a San Francisco shipyard; it started service on August 5, 1887. A year later the Glasgow-built *Islander*, a 1,500-tonne, 12-knot ship, started service but served only 13 years. On August 15, 1901, just after the CPR had taken over the Canadian Pacific Navigation Company, the *Islander* struck an iceberg near Skagway while en route to Vancouver from Alaska and sank with 42 of its 172 passengers and crew.

Union Steamships, formed in 1889, had divided the coastal trade with the CPN, leaving the Vancouver, Victoria, Seattle and Alaska trade to the larger company and serving, instead, the hundreds of smaller settlements.

East of Vancouver the Canadian Pacific built a branch line running south from Mission to provide a joint service with J. J. Hill's Great Northern Railway in the U.S. American prospectors from Idaho and Montana, looking for metals such as lead, copper, zinc, lode gold and silver, had spread into southeastern B.C. in the mid-1880s. Mining these metals demanded large amounts of capital for refineries and a transportation system for the heavy loads of ore. Soon Nelson, Grand Forks, Sandon, New Denver, Rossland and Trail had grown into mining towns of world renown. Unfortunately for the CPR, Hill — a CPR director until 1883 — was close at hand with his Great Northern line. The next few years saw fights, blocked tracks, mergers, bluster, rate-cutting and hurried building of spur lines as the railways fought for access and profits.

Then came the Crowsnest Pass agreement with Ottawa in 1897, in which the CPR got a large subsidy for building a main line to the area through southern Alberta. In return, the railway agreed to carry grain at fixed low rates. The opening of the Crowsnest line not only helped the metal-mining communities, it also gave access to coal in the region. Until then coal had chiefly been mined around Nanaimo on Vancouver Island. Here the chief customers at first were the Royal Navy's Pacific Squadron and the steamships serving the Pacific coast. Demand grew as railway companies switched from wood to coal, and steam engines began to power sawmills, canneries and mines.

The Hudson's Bay Company, first developer of the Nanaimo mines, had sold out to the Vancouver Coal and Land Company, which ran its mines in a paternalistic fashion. Its chief rival was a company run by a former Hudson's Bay mine manager, Robert Dunsmuir. He hired Chinese labourers and ran his mines with a grasping, brutal hand. A strike in 1877 had to be put down by the militia, and the miners went back to work at greatly reduced pay. Dunsmuir and his son James (who succeeded his father in 1889) were in a state of warfare with the miners for most of the rest of the century, and the company's mines were death traps.

The Dunsmuir fortune was made even more secure when the Conservative government in Ottawa gave a syndicate headed by Robert Dunsmuir a contract to build the Esquimalt & Nanaimo Railway in 1886. Like the CPR, it got a massive subsidy and vast land grants.

The forest industry had grown enormously since the first small

Native women and Chinese men operated the fish-packing plants that produced cargoes like this in the 1880s and '90s. Canned B.C. salmon became the main dish of British working-class Sunday teas. As in the lumber and mining industries, large corporations swallowed the small firms until a few controlled the fishing industry.

The first Japanese fisherman came to B.C. in 1871, but serious immigration from Japan did not begin until the 1890s. Most worked as fishermen around Steveston, like the man shown here; others went to farms in the Fraser Valley and the Okanagan.

mills and logging camps started work near Victoria and Yale. By 1861 a New Westminster mill, powered by steam, was exporting dressed lumber to Australia and other markets. By the 1870s, two mills served by six logging camps were at work in Burrard Inlet. Four years before the CPR reached the coast there were more than 20 mills in the province. The railway not only increased demand for lumber for its own track and buildings, it also created new markets in the towns it fostered. Another market opened on the Prairies. The CPR made huge tracts of forest accessible to logging, and soon there was the familiar pattern of mergers, buyouts and the creation of large corporations. The new firms operated stores, hospitals, camps and tugboats and their own spur lines. Vast areas of provincial land were handed over to the forest companies as they demanded more and more raw timber for the mills.

First Nations were barred from commercial fishing when B.C. joined Confederation and Ottawa took over Native affairs, so fishing (in small sailboats using gill nets) became essentially a white man's occupation until the first Japanese arrived in the late 1870s. But in the canneries that were being built in increasing numbers, the workers were a mixture of Native people — mostly women — and Chinese. The fishing industry, chiefly directed to the export trade with Britain (about 60,000 cases of canned salmon went to the United Kingdom in 1877) was seasonal, working only two months of the year.

The first labour unions had been formed in British Columbia in the 1850s by immigrants from Britain working as bakers, shipbuilders and printers. But conditions were not ripe for the growth of unionism until the 1880s, when the Knights of Labor, an early version of the Industrial Workers of the World, moved in from the United States. The Knights of Labor, however, was an industrial union serving all the workers in a plant, not individual crafts. Since there were few large firms, it soon faded. Still, by the mid-1890s there were more than 100 craft union locals in the province, representing painters, builders, masons, carpenters, longshoremen and railway workers. The fishermen's strike of 1900, when a hastily formed group of militiamen had to be shipped to the mouth of the Fraser to protect Japanese fishermen who carried on working, showed that militant unions were now a part of British Columbia's industrial society. The growth of the union movement spurred the growth of political parties and so political life changed, too.

As settlement and industry grew, Native people were pushed more and more out of the mainstream of life in B.C. The industries that suited their skills, such as trapping and fishing, either faded or were denied them. In the other industries — forestry, fish canning and mining — they had to compete with better-positioned Europeans or the Chinese. The missionaries increased their work, usually well-meant but often destructive. Disease and despair were Native people's constant companions. In 1871 there were 26,000 Native people out of a total B.C. population of 36,000. By 1901, 29,000 Native people competed with 179,000 Europeans and Asians. By 1911 there were only 20,000 Native people left.

Emily Carr, painter and author, grew up in a Victoria family of sisters (her brother is not pictured here). Here, in an extract from her The Book of Small, *she's both writer and illustrator as she lovingly recreates a Sunday in those simpler days of the 1880s.*

Emily Carr, bottom right, and her sisters. The Carr family had all the advantages that made for happiness in Victorian society: a masterly father, sufficient wealth to make life comfortable, sisterly affection, loyal servants and an orderly daily routine.

Sunday

All our Sundays were exactly alike. They began on Saturday night after Bong the Chinaboy had washed up and gone away, after our toys, dolls and books, all but *The Peep of Day* and Bunyan's *Pilgrim's Progress*, had been stored away in drawers and boxes till Monday, and every bible and prayerbook in the house was puffing itself out, looking more important every minute.

Then the clothes-horse came galloping into the kitchen and straddled round the stove inviting our clean clothes to mount and be aired. The enormous wooden tub that looked half coffin and half baby-bath was set in the middle of the kitchen floor with a rag mat for dripping on laid close beside it. The great iron soup pot, the copper wash-boiler and several kettles covered the top of the stove, and big sister Dede filled them by working the kitchen pump-handle furiously. It was a sad old pump and always groaned several times before it poured. Dede got the brown windsor soap, heated the towels and put on a thick white apron with a bib. Mother un-buttoned us and by that time the pots and kettles were steaming.

Dede scrubbed hard. If you wriggled, the flat of the long-handled tin dipper came down spankety on your skin.

As soon as each child was bathed Dede took it pick-aback and rushed it upstairs through the cold house. We were allowed to say our prayers kneeling in bed on Saturday night, steamy, brown-windsory prayers — then we cuddled down and tumbled very comfortably into Sunday.

At seven o'clock Father stood beside our bed and said, "Rise up! Rise up! It's Sunday, children." He need not have told us; we knew Father's Sunday smell — Wright's coal-tar soap and camphor. Father had a splendid chest of camphor-wood which had come from England round the Horn in a sailing-ship with him. His clean clothes lived in it and on Sunday he was very camphory ...

Our Sunday dinner was cold saddle of mutton. It was roasted on Saturday in a big tin oven on legs, which was pushed up to the open grate fire in the breakfast room. Father had this fireplace specially built just like the ones in England. The oven fitted right up to it. He thought everything English was much better than anything Canadian. The oven came round the Horn with him, and the big pewter hot water dishes that he ate chops and steaks off, and the heavy mahogany furniture and lots of other things that you could not buy in

Canada then. The tin oven had a jack which you wound up like a clock and it turned the roast on a spit. It said "tick, tick, tick" and turned the meat one way, and then "tock, tock, tock" and turned it the other. The meat sizzled and sputtered. Someone was always opening the little door in the back to baste it, using a long iron spoon, with the dripping that was caught in a pan beneath the meat. Father said no roast under twenty pounds was worth eating because the juice had all run out of it, so it was lucky he had a big family.

THREE

1900 TO 1950

Fighting at Home and Abroad

A mule train outside a store selling supplies for Klondike miners on Vancouver's Cordova Street in 1898. Perhaps the mules were there to carry purchases to the docks nearby. It's more likely, however, that they were part of the store's sales campaign. The gold-rush trade helped to push Vancouver ahead of Victoria as a business centre; money flowed into the city and property values climbed. A lot that sold for $100 in 1887 when the first CPR train arrived was worth $100,000 in 1912. Population in 1892 was 15,000; in 1905 it reached 45,000; by 1910 it had climbed to 98,000.

BIG OUTFIT STARTING FOR KLONDIKE
OHNSTON, KERFOOT & CO'S.
, 104 AND 106 CORDOVA STREET, VANCOUVER, B. C.

You might say the events that shaped British Columbia before 1901 — European exploration, the gold rush, joining Confederation, the arrival of the CPR — were benign compared with those evils that moulded the next 40 years: outbursts of racism, two wars and a shattering Depression.

Since few of us are cursed with a vision of the future, however, the people of British Columbia saw the turn of the century as a time of increasing optimism: more jobs, more investment, more money and better politics.

The squabbling in a system uncontrolled by party discipline had meant that since 1871, petty local issues had dominated the Legislature, made its policies inconsistent and left it open to manipulation by powerful groups. The advent of party politics in 1903 did not mean that suddenly all the bickering and manipulation stopped. The emergence of provincial Conservative, Liberal and Socialist parties did mean that local pressures on legislators, and in particular on premiers, could be diverted by claiming that the party's interests lay elsewhere. And party discipline meant that longer-term policies could be engaged without fear of immediate defeat.

Another cause for optimism: after two decades of indifferent political leadership, a bright, young New Westminster lawyer, Richard McBride, became the first Conservative premier in June 1903. Energetic and intelligent, McBride believed that transportation and an open door for investment were the keys to prosperity in a province so dependent on resources. But first there was the usual demand to Ottawa for more money. Ottawa said provincial taxes were too low and suggested McBride raise them.

There was no shortage of money coming into the province. Americans, Britons and some Europeans believed, like investors from Hong Kong and Japan 80 years later, that British Columbia was a safe and relatively profitable place for their money. The Depression of the last half of the decade was fading away, helped by the Klondike gold rush of 1898. Boarding houses and ships to the north were full, and stores supplying the miners and prospectors were busy all day.

Now American investors and entrepreneurs, not Europeans, dominated the timber industry. The demand caused by the building of railways and the growth of new towns across the American West had stripped Minnesota and Wisconsin of their timber stands, but President Teddy Roosevelt, the energetic outdoorsman who had gone to the White House in 1901, was determined to save the forests and mountains of the United States from the

The right to vote in both provincial and federal elections in B.C. was restricted by the political elite to suit its needs. Women could not vote provincially until 1917, and federally, not until 1918. First Nations and Chinese lost the right to vote in 1874, the Japanese in 1895, and Indians in 1907. Provincial voting rights were restored slowly: Chinese and Indians in 1947; First Nations and Japanese in 1949. Federal voting rights, which were either never granted or were taken away at various times, were given to all of these groups around the same time. Voting rights also governed entrance to certain professions.

J. W. Horne's real-estate office in a hollow log at Georgia and Granville, 1886. There was no mistaking the purpose of life in Vancouver in the early 1900s. In 1908 real-estate firms out-numbered grocery stores three to one. British historian J. A. Hobson wrote after a visit to the city: "It is a purely business town, a thing of stores and banks and meagre wooden houses, with no public buildings of account ... The stranger is amazed at the profusion of solid banking houses; it would almost seem as if the inhabitants must be a race of financiers, concerned purely with money and stocks and shares."

profiteers. In the next few years he put 59 million hectares into national forests. Over the border in Canada, however, there was a government dedicated to creating prosperity and not at all worried about forests and mountains. If firms would agree to operate a sawmill, Victoria would give them 21-year leases of timber for very small rents. In two years after 1901, nearly 15,000 licences were issued. Fortunes were made by speculators and the foundations of the large forest empires were laid.

Men such as American Peter Larson combined railway building with logging and land speculation. Well before the Grand Trunk Pacific had decided on Prince Rupert as its terminus, he bought the land on which Prince Rupert stands. One of his associates was another American, J. H. Bloedel, soon to be a famous name in provincial forests. Through marriage, friendship and business association, a small group of Americans became giants of the forests, bringing money, management skills and the latest techniques. Just before the First World War there were 400 sawmills and more than 800 logging camps at work in the province, and forestry firms paid more than $2.3 million a year in fees and royalties. Company towns sprang up as some firms started to operate mills far from cities but close to water and trees.

Not all the trees in B.C.'s forests were cut to make planks and posts. The demand for wood pulp to make paper to feed the presses of North America, Europe and Japan had prompted the building of pulp mills in eastern Canada in the 1870s. The first attempts to build pulp mills in B.C. came at the turn of the century, but the first successful mill did not start operating until 1909, at Swanson Bay on Vancouver Island. Soon other plants were in operation at Ocean Falls and Powell River, and in April 1912 the *Vancouver Daily Province* started using Powell River newsprint.

H. R. MacMillan, who created Canada's largest forestry company, was born in Ontario in 1885 and came to work in B.C.'s forests in 1907. In 1919, with British money, he created his own lumber-exporting business. To ensure supply he bought mills and, by purchases and mergers, built MacMillan Bloedel Limited. He died in Vancouver in 1976, leaving large bequests to the University of British Columbia.

When war came in 1914, the export trade collapsed and domestic demand fell dramatically, but German submarines sank so many Allied ships that a crash wooden-ship-building program was started. Since about 1.5 million board feet of first-rate lumber was needed for each ship, special logging camps and sawmills opened, and most loggers were working again. Another crash program sent more loggers to work in the Queen Charlottes, cutting spruce so that the aircraft factories of Europe could build Sopwith Camels, SE5s, Spads and other planes for the Billy Bishops of the Allied air forces.

After the war, the industry continued rationalization and turned its energies to marketing. Selling agencies were formed, one in 1919 by H. R. MacMillan, chief provincial forester and federal timber trade commissioner.

MacMillan's was a familiar tale. He came from Ontario in 1907 to work in the B.C. forest industry. During the war he travelled the world, working for both the federal and provincial governments as a salesman for Canadian lumber. After the war he suggested in a report that Victoria set up a peacetime selling agency for British Columbian lumber. It was ignored, so he formed his own export business. The company expanded into the shipping business and soon owned its own mills and camps.

By the late 1920s, the industry was setting production and profitability records. Then the Depression cut output in the province's mills to the lowest mark since 1869. By 1938, however, an active selling campaign had put the industry back to work. When war came again in 1939, the industry was put under government control and prospered, largely because the British market was cut off from its Scandinavian suppliers.

Similar patterns governed the development of the two other major industries of the province, fishing and mining. British money financed mergers and the formation of big fish-packing firms. They started to run their own fishing fleets and built docks and harbours so that larger fishboats could bring in their catches. The boats dropped their sails and installed simple gasoline engines, some built locally. This meant they could go farther afield for more species and enjoy a longer season. Purse seine nets and trolling added to their catches. In the canneries, machinery such as the "iron chink" cut and cleaned the fish and meant 25 workers could do 100 persons' work.

The hard-rock mining industry was largely controlled by American investors. They improved techniques and machinery to meet the demands from the new industries of the American Midwest, such as the automobile factories of Henry Ford and Walter Chrysler.

As industries grew, the significance of agriculture in the economy dwindled. True, the arable parts of the province were cleared,

*B*y the 1920s there was little room for new industrial plants in Vancouver, or so city-boosters pointed out as they tried to shuck off its image as a frontier town interested only in lumber and fish. More than 1,000 industrial plants were operating, with 27,000 workers producing $100 million worth of goods a year. Fifty steamship lines used the docks. Foundries, steel works, pulp and paper plants, printing, shipbuilding — these were just a few of Vancouver's industries. The promoters did not mention that only 8 percent of the industrial products was not linked to resource industries, a figure that hardly changed for many years.

cultivated and brought into production, with emphasis on supplying the growing cities and suburbs with milk, fresh vegetables and fruit. Ranchers started running cattle on the dry land around Kamloops and in the Cariboo. Most food, however, was imported.

Immigrants and investors, attracted by the climate of the Okanagan valley and the potential of the land once it was irrigated, flowed into the area. Some immigrants tried to recreate Edwardian England, just as the first settlers had tried to establish midcentury England around Victoria. Coyotes replaced foxes for hunting, English-style, and cricket joined tennis as the sport for the genteel. For those with fewer social aspirations there were soccer and lacrosse.

Work in the fish canneries was usually divided on sexist and racist lines. Chinese men gutted and cut the fish, Native women trimmed and canned it. The invention in 1900 of a mechanical gutter with a steel belly filled with knives and iron brushes, nicknamed the "iron chink," cut the Chinese workforce drastically.

If one railway — the CPR — had made money and brought prosperity to British Columbia, then more railways would bring even more. That's the way the thinking went. Research into potential demand and rigorous costing was not wanted. If there

The CPR sprouted branch lines to the south in the 1890s and so encouraged development in areas such as the Okanagan Valley and the Kootenays. In the Okanagan, fruit-growing prospered, as this Kelowna apple-orchard photograph shows. The days of mechanical pickers and containers were still to come — as were the vineyards.

were generous governments and foolish investors, then it was time to build a railway.

There were to be two more transcontinental railways. One, the Grand Trunk Pacific, was to extend from Winnipeg across northern Manitoba, Saskatchewan, Alberta and British Columbia to Prince Rupert. It was incorporated in 1903 and built in eight years, from 1906 to 1914. It never made money and dragged down its parent firm, the Grand Trunk Railway, which had operated in Quebec and Ontario since 1852. The GTP was taken over by the federal government in 1919 and incorporated into Canadian National Railways in 1923.

William Mackenzie and Donald Mann were the promoters of the second railway — the Canadian Northern Pacific. They persuaded Premier Richard McBride to sign a contract with them without the approval of his cabinet on October 9, 1909. McBride offered financial help and massive land grants and was so generous that Mackenzie and Mann used the spare cash to buy a large coal company. The Canadian Northern's route crossed the Prairies

Canadian Pacific Railway
Canadian National Railway
Grand Trunk Pacific Railway
Pacific Great Eastern Railway

Hazelton

Prince Rupert

Fort St. James

Prince George

ALBERTA

BRITISH COLUMBIA

Quesnel

To Edmonton
via Yellowhead Pass

Williams Lake

Kicking Horse Pass
To Calgary

Fraser River

Golden

Craigellachie

Squamish

Kamloops

Vancouver
Nanaimo
Spences Bridge

Crowsnest Pass

Keremeos

Victoria
Hope
Trail

Pacific Ocean

U.S.A.

The early 20th century was B.C.'s boom time for new railways. The Grand Trunk Pacific and the Canadian Northern were national but lasted only a few years. The third, the provincial Pacific Great Eastern, is now B.C. Rail and alive and well. For Premier Richard McBride, provincial support for the Pacific section of the Canadian Northern was not enough; in 1912 he authorized provincial bonds to finance the building of the Pacific Great Eastern to help the Canadian Northern by linking Burrard Inlet with the northern Interior. Construction was bedevilled by scandal, and critics said the railway was merely a disguised Tory campaign fund, and only parts of the line (North Vancouver to Horseshoe Bay and Squamish to Clinton) were built when the government took it over in 1919.

and used the Yellowhead Pass rejected by the CPR. Then it ran down the Fraser Canyon, usually on the other side of the river from the CPR. The last spike was driven at Ashcroft in the summer of 1915, and the first train arrived in Vancouver in October, using Great Northern tracks. Like the Grand Trunk Pacific, the Canadian Northern's construction was a sad tale of blunders and financial chicanery, but government purses had run dry, and the line was bankrupt before it reached Vancouver. The Canadian Northern, too, was folded into Canadian National in 1918.

The growth of big business led to the growth of big unions. Militant labour groups such as the Industrial Workers of the World ("Wobblies") came in from the United States before the 1914 war and formed branches here. They attracted railwaymen, miners and other workers in industries where wages and conditions were bad.

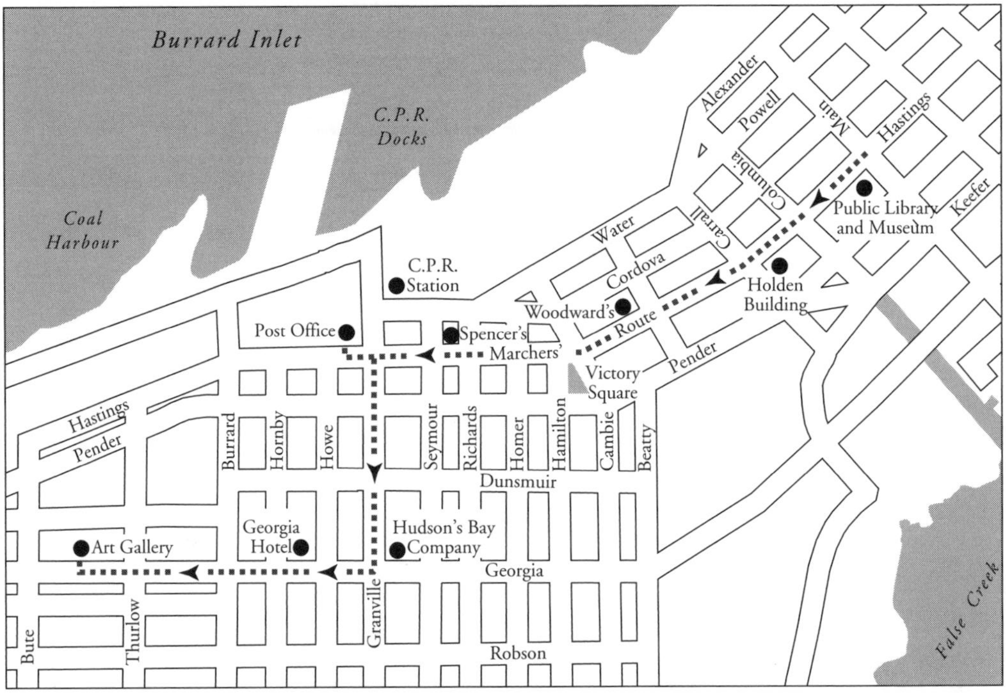

Burrard Inlet

C.P.R. Docks

Coal Harbour

C.P.R. Station

Post Office

Alexander
Powell
Main
Hastings
Columbia
Carrall

Public Library and Museum
Keefer

Holden Building

Water
Cordova
Woodward's
Route
Spencer's
Marchers'
Victory Square
Pender

Hastings
Pender
Burrard
Hornby
Howe
Seymour
Richards
Homer
Hamilton
Cambie
Beatty
Dunsmuir

Georgia Hotel
Hudson's Bay Company
Georgia

Art Gallery

Bute
Thurlow
Granville
Robson

False Creek

During the Depression, Vancouver's warm climate attracted the jobless from across Canada. Attempts to herd people into camps in the Interior failed. Neglected by the political parties and the trade unions, the men listened to new leaders and were soon surging, out of control, through the city streets. The above map of Vancouver shows sites of riots.

The Wobblies regarded political action as valueless and placed more emphasis on demonstrations and strikes. There was no shortage of targets for them. Thousands of workers were demanding better pay and conditions. In 1910 there were strikes in mines, the fishing industry and among construction gangs building the Grand Trunk Pacific and Canadian Northern railways. More work stoppages plagued construction of the Grand Trunk Pacific's terminus at Prince Rupert in 1911, and sailors from the Royal Canadian Navy were called in to restore order. A strike in 1911 involving labourers building the Canadian Northern's tracks down the Fraser Canyon was put down harshly, and strike leaders were given stiff jail sentences. In 1913 coal miners at Cumberland, near Nanaimo, went on strike. Japanese and Chinese workers were brought in, and the strikers rioted in Nanaimo, wrecking buildings and terrorizing the town. Militiamen were called in to help the police and stayed on guard until the First World War broke out in August 1914.

Party Politics

Before 1903 no political party system existed. Premiers depended on the support of changing coalitions.

1903	McBride/Cons	1941	Hart/Coalition	1991	Harcourt/NDP
1915	Bowser/Cons	1947	Johnson/Coalition	1996	Clark/NDP
1916	Brewster/Lib	1952	Bennett/Socred	1999	Miller/NDP
1918	Oliver/Lib	1972	Barrett/NDP	2000	Dosanjh/NDP
1927	MacLean/Lib	1975	Bennett/Socred	2001	Campbell/Lib
1928	Tolmie/Cons	1986	Vander Zalm/Socred		
1933	Pattullo/Lib	1991	Johnston/Socred		

Conservatives became Progressive Conservatives in 1942.
The Cooperative Commonwealth Federation became the New Democratic Party in 1961.

Popular Vote
Until 1933 Conservatives and Liberals split about 90 percent of the popular vote. In 1933 the CCF Opposition won 32 percent to Duff Patullo's 42. Since then the CCF/NDP Opposition vote has ranged from 46 percent (1979) to 28 percent (1956) and down to 23 percent in 2001. Socreds won 0.4 percent in 1949 but increased their rate to 30 percent in 1952 — enough to gain more seats than the CCF with a 34 percent popular vote. Dave Barrett won with 40 percent in 1972 and lost with 39 percent in 1975.

In Vancouver in 1918, uncontrolled high food prices were the reason for stoppages involving longshoremen, streetcar workers and city employees. On August 2 there was a massive strike in Vancouver to protest the police killing of Albert "Ginger" Goodwin, a union organiser, wanted for evading conscription. Servicemen just back from France started a counterprotest and jumped on streetcars to force drivers to stay on the streets and not go back to the depot.

Later, the Depression was to crush the labour movement so that by 1934 only seven percent of B.C. workers were in unions. As the war came and factories opened again, union membership

*Albert "Ginger" Goodwin, a
labour organizer, was shot by
police outside Cumberland
on July 27, 1918. He was 31.
On August 7, the day of his
funeral, union members in
Vancouver started a general
strike and fought with
returning servicemen who
sided with employers.
Goodwin's friends
maintained that he had been
gunned down not because he
had tried to avoid military
service and arrest, but
because of his record as a
strike leader in the Kootenays.*

increased and reached 30 percent in the middle of the war.
Workers' associations such as the Trades and Labour Congress and
Canadian Congress of Labour grew more powerful and started
recruitment drives in agriculture and service industries.

British Columbia's political culture was formed in the first
quarter of the century. The major parties, Conservatives and
Liberals, viewed the creation of wealth as all-important, and in
the first 25 years they made certain that entrepreneurs lacked
nothing. Land, financial help, benign legislation and the use of
the police or the military to control workers when necessary — all
of these were handed out by the government, so long as jobs were
created and investors got dividends.

Naturally, this kind of politics caused an equal and opposite
reaction. Since the 1930s, labour unions, reform movements and
parties promoting greater power for the state and a gentler society challenged the old-line alliances in a seemingly perpetual
polarization.

Premier McBride was an extrovert, a glad-hander who toured
the province and exuded optimism. He was helped at first by a
booming economy and the fad for railways, but by 1914 his railway
deals were duds, the economy slowed and his vision lost its gleam.
Ill with a disabling kidney disease, McBride resigned in 1915 and
went to London as a special envoy to help the war effort. He died
soon after he arrived there.

McBride's successor had the unfortunate name of Bowser
(William John) and lasted less than a year. By 1916, a 60-30 split
of the popular vote for the Tories had become a 50-40 split for the
Liberals, and they took power. But their new leader, Harlan
Brewster, died after less than two years in the premier's office and
was succeeded in 1918 by a colleague, John Oliver.

Oliver was a political backroom-man's dream. He had worked
in the coal mines in England, come to Canada, taken various jobs
and then become an honest man of the soil, running a successful
pig farm in Delta. Where McBride had a vision of railways,
"Honest John" had a vision of dirt and ditches. Convinced that

$500 Reward

The above reward will be paid for the arrest and detention of **WILLIAM (Bill) MINER**, alias Edwards, who escaped from the New Westminster Penitentiary, at New Westminster, British Columbia, on the 8th August, 1907, where he was serving a life sentence for train robbery.

DESCRIPTION:

Age 65 years; 138 pounds; 5 feet 8½ inches; dark complexion; brown eyes; grey hair; slight build; face spotted; tattoo base of left thumb, star and ballet girl right forearm; wrist joint-bones large; moles centre of breast, 1 under left breast, 1 on right shoulder, 1 on left shoulder-blade; discoloration left buttock; scars on left shin, right leg, inside, at knee, 2 on neck.

Communicate with

LT.-COL. A. P. SHERWOOD,

Commissioner Dominion Police,
Ottawa, Canada.

Newspaper accounts of crime intrigued readers then as now. On September 10, 1904, Bill Miner, just released from San Quentin prison in the U.S., held up a CPR transcontinental train near Mission and escaped with cash by rowing across the Fraser River. Less than two years later, on May 14, 1906, Miner held up another train but was chased by a posse and captured near Kamloops. He was sentenced to 25 years in New Westminster Penitentiary but escaped in August 1907 and fled to the States, where he died in 1913.

Premier Thomas Dufferin "Duff" Pattullo woos a future voter. Pattullo, Liberal premier from 1933 to 1941, lived a long, exciting life. Born in 1873, he was a journalist in Ontario before he went to the Yukon and served as a government administrator until 1902, then went into business in Dawson City and later Prince Rupert. Elected to the B.C. Legislature in 1916, he became minister of lands. After a spell in opposition, he became premier in the middle of the Depression.

agriculture was the key to the province's prosperity, he drained Sumas Prairie and irrigated large tracts of the Okanagan. More big tracts of land in the Peace River region were sold to would-be farmers. But cancer killed Oliver in 1927, and his successor, John MacLean, another unknown, lasted a year.

It was the Tories' turn again. Simon Fraser Tolmie — can there be a better name for a B.C. politician? — became premier. He was a veterinarian and Conservative MP for Victoria. Tolmie returned to British Columbia to help the provincial party select a new leader. None could be found, so Tolmie got the job. The Depression was the death of better politicians than Tolmie, and he showed little understanding of the economic catastrophe that had struck the province.

In the 1933 election the reaction was obvious. Liberal Duff Pattullo, an admirer of President Roosevelt's New Deal policies, became premier with 42 percent of the popular vote. The Conservatives disappeared in a flurry of splinter parties and the new Cooperative Commonwealth Federation won 32 percent, though only seven seats to Pattullo's 34. Pattullo tried to improve welfare payments, started agricultural stabilization boards, built bridges and improved the lot of the poor and jobless, but his left-wing opponents accused him of trying to put a smile on the face of capitalism. He did little for the unemployed and homeless, they said, forgetting that Pattullo's powers were limited and that Ottawa took refuge in doing nothing.

By 1937 the Conservatives had formed lines again and were challenging the CCF as the Opposition. Pattullo won the election but should have seen the crisis coming. In 1941 the CCF increased its popular vote, and right-wing Liberals, concerned at the left-wing surge, joined with the Conservatives and kicked Pattullo out. New Liberal leader John Hart became head of a coalition government that stayed in power, with different leaders, until the 1950s. But there were signs — true, no bigger than a man's hand — of future conflicts: one of the CCF members of the Legislature was Frank Calder, a Nisga'a.

When they weren't coping with wars, economic slumps, strikes and the chicanery and stupidity of their politicians, British Columbians found time to enjoy themselves. Vancouver's first theatre, Hart's Opera House, had opened in 1887 on Carrall Street and in a couple of years there were 10 more. Others entertained crowds in Victoria and the Kootenay towns. Plays and musicals were on the bills at first; then came vaudeville companies with stars such as Charlie Chaplin and Stan Laurel. Polish pianist (and later president) Ignace Paderewski played at the Opera House. Diaghilev's Ballet Russe, with Nijinsky as the star, entertained Vancouver's elite on January 15, 1917. Some theatres added a moving picture to the bill, and gradually American movies pushed the live actors offstage.

Jazz and later swing bands played for dancers in hotel ballrooms and clubs. The public's appetite for this music was sharpened by the "big band" radio programs of Paul Whiteman, Benny Goodman, Tommy Dorsey and others broadcast from Seattle stations.

Canadian radio was dominated at first, like so much else, by

First-year university courses, sponsored by McGill University in Montreal, were first offered to Vancouver students in 1899. Work on a provincial university on the present site was stopped when war began in 1914 and was slow in resuming when the war ended. After a protest march by students in 1925, the provincial government freed funds, and the Point Grey campus of the University of British Columbia opened in 1926. As this aerial view shows, it is now the size of a small city.

Theatres quickly opened in the prosperous, brash city of Vancouver. The Opera House, next to the Hotel Vancouver, opened in 1891 with the backing of the CPR. The Pantages Theatre (shown here) featured plays, musicals, vaudeville and, finally, movies.

the railways, for whom it was another kind of communication, like the telegraph. But by the 1920s, private, individual stations were operating in Vancouver.

On Sundays the churches and their Sunday schools dictated most families' activities and tried to lay a veneer of gentility over the harshness of life in a still immature province. Bars were everywhere and brothels were tucked away discreetly in selected districts. The brothels were not talked about in society but drinking was, and reform movements led by the churches and women's

A few days after Prohibition became law in the U.S., enterprising B.C. seamen converted boats to take Canadian-distilled booze across Juan de Fuca Strait and down the coast. They were workers in a miniature market system run by dealers who set up depots, sold to other dealers and organized delivery runs. Dealers paid smugglers $11 a case; a small fishboat could carry 75 cases. Slower boats would leave their B.C. depots in late morning so their run through U.S. waters was in the dark. Other specially built boats sported Packard and Fiat aero engines and could easily outrun U.S. Coast Guard boats in daylight. But danger came from hijackers, not the coast guard. In September 1924 a small depot ship, the *Beryl G.*, was ransacked and sunk off Sidney Island. Its crew, William Gillis and his son, were killed. In January 1926 two men were hanged for the murders at Oakalla prison, in Burnaby.

groups attacked the problems caused by cheap and easily obtainable beer and spirits.

In 1916 women celebrated a double victory: bars and booze were outlawed, and women were given the provincial vote (they won the federal vote in 1918). But the bars opened again in 1921, and the government took over the sale of liquor.

Over the border, drinkers were not so fortunate, and British Columbian distillers and distributors made fortunes as they sold hootch to the thirsty Americans. Coal Harbour in Vancouver and the Gulf Islands were the home bases of the rum-running trade as speedboats supplied the northern Pacific coast, and tenders from mother ships tried to satisfy dry Californians. Other adventurers drove big cars loaded with liquor over the border.

Helen Gregory MacGill was the first woman to graduate from Trinity College in Toronto and she then became a reporter and foreign correspondent. Born in 1864 in Hamilton, in 1903 she came to Vancouver and in 1917 was named the first female judge in western Canada. For most of her life she fought for reform in the status of women and for more sympathetic treatment of children. Her daughter, Elizabeth, was the first female graduate in electrical engineering from the University of Toronto and became an aeronautical engineer, designer of the Maple Leaf training plane.

This was the time when newspapers flourished on competition. In Victoria, the *British Colonist* and the *Victoria Times* had been informing and badgering the people of the capital for 50 years or more. In New Westminster, John Robson, an ardent Confederationist and later premier, had founded the *British Columbian* at around the same time.

The newspaper trade in Vancouver, following the patterns of the forestry and fishing industries, saw mergers, buyouts and bankruptcies as the *Advertiser, News Advertiser, World, Daily Province, Telegram, Sun, Star* and *News Herald* jostled for business. In the 1920s the two strongest newspapers, the *Sun* and *Daily Province,* competed for readers and advertisements in ways that made Vancouver an exciting town for both readers and journalists.

So far this has been a story about making money, enjoyment, fighting for political power and raising families. Now it becomes a story about the darker side — racism, wars and the Depression.

British Columbia at the turn of the century was Little England. The attitude among those from Britain was that the best immigrants came from the Old Country. Americans ranked next, and then other Europeans. People whose skins were not white and who worshipped different gods were beyond the pale.

The Wah Chong family in Vancouver in 1884. Despite discrimination and violence, the tightly knit Chinese community survived and prospered. This pioneer family lived on Water Street between Abbott and Carrall in what was, in effect, a clearing in the forest. Jennie Wah Chong was the first Chinese child to attend school in the city.

The first Chinese had come to British Columbia with John Meares in 1788 but did not stay. In 1858 some Chinese from the United States joined the gold rush and then settled. They were joined by large numbers in the 1880s as the railways made deals with Chinese contractors to import cheap labour. When railway work finished, the Chinese became shopkeepers, farmers, servants and laundrymen and set up settlements in the towns.

The first Japanese man came in 1878. Others followed in the early 1880s and worked as fishermen and in sawmills and on farms. They, too, stayed, started families and formed their own settlements at Steveston on the Fraser River and on Powell Street in Vancouver.

Sikhs also started coming in the 1880s as shipping service between the Orient and Vancouver began. Back home they were loggers and farmers, and they worked in British Columbia in the same trades.

All these groups came to British Columbia seeking the same thing: decent-paying work, not easily obtained in their homelands with rising populations and limited industrialization.

The elite of British Columbia and their working-class allies did their best to keep Asians out of the country and to make their lives miserable if they got in. A series of laws and administrative devices were aimed at non-white immigrants. Egged on by newspapers, pressure groups and workers worried about cheap labour, the Legislature introduced head taxes, quotas, literacy tests and restricted job opportunities. Most, but not all, of these crudely disguised tricks were rejected by Ottawa or the courts.

When politics failed, there was always violence. Vancouver had its first race riot on February 24, 1887, when it was less than a year old. A mob wrecked a camp in False Creek full of Chinese labourers just laid off by the CPR. On September 7, 1907, another mob listened to speeches at an Asiatic Exclusion League meeting and

Sikhs wait aboard the Komogata Maru *in Vancouver harbour in July 1914. Arriving in the freighter chartered by a wealthy Sikh businessman, they were forbidden to land, and after skirmishes with officials, the rusty old cruiser HMCS Rainbow was called in to stand guard. Eventually the 354 barred Sikhs sailed home. The trip was undoubtedly an attempt to test Canadian immigration laws.*

Just before the war ended, on October 28, 1918, the CPR's Princess Sophia ran onto a reef just out of Skagway on a voyage to Vancouver. For three days the 340 passengers and crew waited for rescue, but the weather was too bad. Suddenly the ship slipped off the rock and went down with everyone on board. In peacetime the news would have filled the newspapers and been the subject of talk for days, but Allied troops were close to victory in France and the Spanish flu epidemic was raging (522 cases were reported in Vancouver on October 27).

stormed off to wreck Chinatown. The rioters met little resistance. They moved to Little Tokyo but found the Japanese, proud of their Imperial Navy's trouncing of Russia in the 1905 war, less submissive. Fighting broke out until a truce was called. Two days after the attack there was a general strike of all Chinese workers, and many matrons had to do their own washing.

By the 1920s, the racists had won. Immigration of non-whites was just a trickle and stayed that way for 30 years.

When war came in August 1914, there were only two small sloops and the old-fashioned cruiser HMCS *Rainbow* to defend the Pacific coast. Out in the Pacific, it was believed, lurked a German cruiser squadron ready to sink ships and attack Vancouver. As a quick fix the province bought two submarines, built for the Chilean navy, from a Seattle shipyard and then handed them over to the Royal Canadian Navy. Coastal defence guns were hastily installed at Point Grey to protect Burrard Inlet and at Stanley Park to protect the harbour. A detachment of 300 men was sent to Prince Rupert to protect the new harbour there, but no German raiders came, and after a few months it was obvious that the Pacific coast would not see any action.

Most of the immigrants who had come to the province in the

previous 30 years or so were from Britain. In those days patriotism was a simpler affair, and thousands of British Columbians were soon on their way to Britain to train for the trenches and die by their thousands in France. Back in Vancouver, the men who stayed and thousands of women started work in shipyards, machine shops and munition factories. The sinking of the liner *Lusitania* by a German submarine off the Irish coast on May 24, 1915, led to anti-German riots in Victoria. Hotels and shops with German names or believed to be owned by Germans were attacked.

When war came again, just 20 years later, the inlet and the harbour were protected by two groups of six-inch naval guns at Point Grey and Stanley Park. Emplacements with searchlights and listening posts were built, but the guns never fired. In 1942 an American freighter was torpedoed off Vancouver Island and the naval station at Estevan Point was shelled by a Japanese submarine, but the great naval and land battles of the Pacific war were being fought thousands of kilometres away.

The first migrations from Europe to Canada were of working-class or peasant people. Few jobs, low pay and an oppressive social or religious climate at home made life in Canada seem attractive and worth the cost and hardships of crossing the Atlantic.

In the early 1900s migration moved upscale. Young sons of British families who saw little chance of inheriting estates or titles joined land societies that bought and began to develop settlements in the Interior of B.C.

One of these was Walhachin, beside the railroad between Cache Creek and Kamloops and designed to be a little garden city. Irrigation flumes were built to carry water from the hills to the dry and dusty plain. Orchards were planted, homes, stores, clubhouses and stables were built. Population in 1914: 150.

But as soon as war broke out 43 men left for France. One story is that the women and older men who stayed could not care for the flumes, orchards and gardens. Another is that the comminity was poorly planned and run and would have died even if war had not come. At any rate, when a few men returned after the war the sagebrush once again covered the land.

Two members of the pacifist Russian Doukhobor sect that settled in southeastern B.C. in 1908. About 6,000 people started a rural communal life, but it was soon split by dissent and some families bought private homes. The breakaway Sons of Freedom group burned schools to protest provincial compulsory education. Eventually, the community's land was taken over by the province. There was more protest and resistance to government authority from 1950 to 1960, but now the province's Doukhobors focus on keeping their cultural and religious heritage alive.

In Vancouver and Victoria, the shipyards worked to capacity and hired more than 30,000 people to build freighters and small naval ships. The race to join the armed forces was less eager than in 1914, but large numbers of men were soon in Europe. Some died at Dieppe or in their bombers over Germany, but most had to wait until 1944 before they met the Germans on the beaches of Normandy. Back home, women built ships and airplanes and made electrical equipment for guns, ships and planes. When peace came, they mostly followed the examples set by their mothers in 1918 and stayed home to rear children.

Fifty years of discrimination against Japanese immigrants and their Canadian-born children came to a head in the winter of 1941–42. Soon after the Japanese attacked Pearl Harbor in December 1941, Japanese fishermen were rounded up and their boats were seized.

Early in 1942, 20,881 Japanese-Canadians were expelled from their homes on the coast. Some men were sent to work on highways in the Interior. Families were interned in the horse and cattle barns at Hastings Park, with little privacy and shameful

Strikes and Violence in B.C.

1850: Fort Rupert coal miners.

Turn of the century: Nanaimo coal miners; Fraser fishermen; Kootenay miners; Canadian Pacific Railway workers.

1910: Railway workers; coal miners.

1910: The B.C. Federation of Labour was formed. The Industrial Workers of the World "Wobblies") were very active in this period.

1911: Grand Trunk Pacific railroad workers at Prince Rupert; Crowsnest coal miners.

1913: Nanaimo coal miners.

1917: Crowsnest miners.

1918: Vancouver longshoremen; shipyard workers; transit workers; Vancouver general strike.

1919: Vancouver workers support Winnipeg general strike.

1929-1939: Depression.

1952: B.C. woodworkers.

1983: Solidarity versus Bill Bennett.

sanitary conditions. Some families were sent to work on sugar-beet farms in Alberta and Manitoba, and others were taken to camps in southeastern B.C. The seized property they left behind was sold at ridiculously low prices, and little of the cash found its way back to them.

When the campaign against the Japanese began, the RCMP, army and navy said the Japanese posed no danger. It was obvious that the expulsion was generated by locally fomented racism and resentment of Japanese prosperity. Many British Columbia politicians and society leaders had led the attack. Others chose "discretion" over principle. National security was never at risk. When the war ended, unrepentant Ottawa tried to deport the Japanese but, after a few had been sent back, gave up.

Between the two wars came the Great Depression. The conventional story of the Depression of the 1930s goes like this: after a time of extravagance and pleasure-seeking, of booze and short

Fishboats owned by Japanese-Canadians and seized by the Royal Canadian Navy after the attack on Pearl Harbor in December, 1941, are moored near Steveston before being sold. Racism, never far from the surface in Vancouver at the time, and fanned by politicians, resulted in charges of espionage and treason against Japanese-Canadians. Fishboats were seized and, later, families interned. The high cost of "reconditioning" (often unnecessary) and other charges were deducted from the money paid the owners, usually a fraction of the vessels' true worth.

skirts and stockings rolled above the knee, the economy collapsed and hard times were had by all.

The reality, particularly in B.C., is somewhat different. The 1920s were not only the time of the flapper. They were also the time of soup kitchens in the cities and poverty in the Interior. Forestry and mining were prospering, but the fishing industry still felt the effects of the Hells Gate slide of 1913, when dynamiting by contractors building the Canadian Northern Railway sent tonnes of rock into the Fraser River and well-nigh destroyed the sockeye salmon run. There was no plan to absorb the thousands of discharged servicemen seeking jobs, and wartime factories stayed silent.

On October 29, 1929, the stock exchange crash reverberated through North America and Europe. Orders were cancelled, loans called, factories shut and workers sent home. Prime Minister Mackenzie King said, "business was never better." But almost everyone except the politicians and a few shortsighted businessmen knew otherwise, particularly in British Columbia. Two

months into the Depression, eight days before Christmas, unemployed men were besieging a Vancouver relief office.

Number-gathering was not the science it is today, and no one knows how many lost their jobs and sought relief. Best estimates are that in the City of Vancouver, for example, 8,000 families were on relief and 40,000 were "just hanging on." About 28 percent of workers were unemployed. Across Canada, 1.35 million were on relief.

Another conventional image is that a blanket of gloom stretched over the land. The truth is that there were pockets, if small indeed, of comfort and happiness, and the misery of British Columbia was nothing compared with that of the Atlantic provinces. If a husband in B.C. kept his job, life was comfortable, for prices were low (a hamburger cost 10 cents, a movie 50 cents), maids would work for almost nothing and rents were cheap.

But for the jobless, the old and poor, life was hard. There were none of the systems of today that may bring money and some security to people hit by economic distress. There was no employment

Female soldiers parade in Hastings Park in Vancouver, 1915. Women have often gone to war, usually as camp followers or nurses, but they enlisted as soldiers for the first time in the 1914–18 war. In the Canadian army they "freed" men for combat in France.

ABOVE: During the Depression there were many sights like this. For the person without a job, home or family, there was often only the park bench and the realization that tomorrow would be no better, perhaps worse.

NEXT PAGE: The Depression struck the suburbs of Vancouver very differently. In 1930 West Vancouver recorded only 20 unemployed, but soon, there was work for everyone as land was prepared for British...

insurance, no social security system underwritten by Ottawa and run by the provinces. Relief came from the municipalities, and they did not have the resources to cope with poverty on this massive level. The municipality of West Vancouver was barely affected, but the other municipalities around Vancouver went bankrupt despite help from the provincial and federal governments and were taken over by commissioners.

All the attention was focused on the single males who protested, rioted, were put in relief and forestry camps and demanded money. Forgotten were the old, particularly old Chinese people, and single women living away from their families.

Most politicians did little, for they believed that the capitalist system that had survived downturns in the past would soon rebound. Spending money on relief and work projects was in their view not only unnecessary, it was foolish. Balanced budgets were the key to economic growth.

Fortunately, John Maynard Keynes, a culture-loving English

Depression Statistics

Spring 1930: 7,000 people on relief in Vancouver. 1932: 8,000 of Burnaby's 25,000 population out of work.
February 1933: 100,000 jobless in Vancouver, in a population of 694,000.
March 1933: 1.36 million Canadians on relief.

There was no accurate system of measuring unemployment, the workforce or welfare recipients. Neither was there unemployment insurance. Relief, run by municipal and provincial governments, churches and private institutions, was largely based on the thesis that unemployment and poverty were self-inflicted and sinful.

Pacific Properties, controlled by the Guinness brewing family. Access to the exclusive residential suburb was to be via a bridge across Burrard Inlet at First Narrows, but winning approval to build a roadway through Stanley Park took time and the Lions Gate Bridge, shown here in a view from the water, was not built until 1938. It cost $6 million and tolls were charged until 1963, when the province bought the span.

civil servant turned Cambridge economist, was prompted into writing his *General Theory of Employment, Interest and Money,* which showed that the reality was far more complex: government could get an economy moving again. His theories set the standards for a return to prosperity after the war.

Labour unions had no place for unemployed members, and so it was natural for the jobless to listen to new leaders and to organizations such as the Workers Unity League, mostly led by Communists.

British Columbia's climate lured the jobless and homeless from across the country, and young single men, riding the rail freight cars to the coast, added to the numbers seeking food, money and a place to sleep. Municipal and provincial politicians demanded help from Ottawa and, after long delays and pompous speeches from Prime Minister R. B. Bennett, some came. Relief and forestry camps were built in the Interior to get the unemployed out of Vancouver. With low pay, poor food and no women, the camps were breeding grounds for riots, if not revolt, and many of the men flocked back to Vancouver.

Leaders of the unemployed organized protests to get public attention and to frighten the already terrified politicians. There

On May 20, 1938, about 1,200 unemployed men evaded police cordons and occupied the old art gallery on Georgia Street in Vancouver, the Hotel Georgia and the old post office at Granville and Hastings. City politicians bribed the men to leave the art gallery and the Hotel Georgia, but those in the post office stayed until June 20, when the police used tear gas to force them out.

was a march of 15,000 people through Vancouver in March 1932. On April 23, 1935, about 1,400 people occupied the Hudson's Bay store at Georgia and Granville. When they were forced out, the men marched to Victory Square, and Mayor Gerry McGeer read the Riot Act.

On May 16 the men occupied the City Library at Hastings and Main and then decided to ride the trains to Ottawa, but when they reached Regina, their camp was surrounded by troops and police.

The best-planned and biggest act of defiance came on May 20, 1938, when 700 men evaded the police and slipped into the post office at Granville and Hastings. Another 300 took over the Hotel Georgia and 200 quietly moved into the art gallery on Georgia. Those in the Hotel Georgia left after being paid money by city aldermen, but many of those in the post office and art gallery

Victoria's old Legislative Building, called "the Birdcages," was designed by Herman Tiedemann and built to house the first Legislature, moved from New Westminster to Victoria in 1868. Francis Rattenbury's new building, which still houses the legislature today, was opened 30 years later. The peculiar name? Some say early settlers from England remembered that the road from Parliament to Buckingham Palace was called Birdcage Walk. Others say the building's elaborate decoration reminded them of the birdcages then fashionable.

stayed until the early morning of Sunday, June 20, when they were ejected by the RCMP with tear gas.

Nothing really changed for a year, and then the war came. Strangely, money was found to feed and house the men — and give them work to do.

Soon after Japanese planes attacked Pearl Harbor in December 1941, the Royal Canadian Navy seized the boats of Japanese-Canadian fishermen. Early in 1942 about 21,000 Japanese-Canadian men, women and children were expelled from their homes in the Lower Mainland. Most were taken to Hastings Park and lodged in the agricultural fair barns there.

Muriel Kitigawa was a writer for a United Church newspaper for young Nisei (those born in Canada of Japanese descent). She wrote a series of letters to her brother, Wesley, a medical student in Toronto. Here's one from This is My Own:

Japanese-Canadian men start their journey in 1942 from Vancouver to internment camps in the Interior or farms on the Prairies. Photographs taken by Vancouver newspapers or the police, like this one, usually show calm dignity. Photographs taken by Japanese families, now in archives, show distress and fear.

Hastings Park Description
April 20, 1942

Dear Wes:

Eiko sleeps in a partitioned stall, she being on the staff, so to speak. This stall was the former home of a pair of stallions and boy oh boy, did they leave their odour behind. The whole place is impregnated with the smell of ancient manure and maggots. Every other day it is swept with dichloride of lime or something, but you can't disguise horse smell, cow smell, sheep and pigs and rabbits and goats. And is it dusty! The toilets are just a sheet metal trough, and up till now they did not have partitions or seats. The women kicked so they put up partitions and a terribly makeshift seat. Twelve-year-old boys stay with the women too. As for the bunks, they were the most tragic things I saw there. Steel and wooden frames with a thin lumpy straw tick, a bolster and three army blankets of army quality ... no sheets unless you bring your own. These are the "homes" of the women I saw. They wouldn't let me into the men's building. There are constables at the doors ... no propagation of the species ... you know ... it was in the papers. These bunks were hung with sheets and blankets and clothes of every hue and variety, a regular gipsy tent of colours, age and cleanliness, all hung with the pathetic attempt at privacy. Here and there I saw a child's doll and teddy bear ... I saw babies lying there beside a mother who was too weary to get up ... she had just thrown herself across the bed ... I felt my throat thicken ... an old, old lady was crying, saying she would rather have died than have come to such a place ... she clung to Eiko and cried and cried. Eiko has taken the woes of the confinees on her thin shoulders and she took so much punishment she went to her former rooms and couldn't stop crying. Fumi was so worried about her. Eiko is really sick. The place has got her down. There are ten showers for fifteen-hundred women. Hot and cold water. The men looked so terribly at loose ends, wandering around the grounds, sticking their noses through the fence watching the golfers, lying on the grass. Going through the place I felt so depressed that I wanted to cry. I'm damned well not going there. They are going to move the Vancouver women first now and shove them into the Pool before sending them to the ghost towns.

With love,
Mur

FOUR

1950 TO 1986

At Last, the Good Life

Before he became premier, Bennett had pressed in the Legislature for an extension of the Pacific Great Eastern Railway. It was the best way to spur development in northern B.C., he said. Under his rule the railway reached Prince George and was then extended north to the Peace River district and south from Squamish to North Vancouver. Bennett never rejected a chance to celebrate, and here he is enjoying the opening of the extension to Prince George.

Until now this history of British Columbia has focused on events. Strong personalities — men like Sir James Douglas and others — played their roles, but events outshone the players. After the Second World War, however, it seemed that events became less significant and personalities more. The growth of mass media, and other factors, helped make strong characters and single-issue groups the dominant features of public life.

One man, William Andrew Cecil Bennett, ruled public life in British Columbia from 1952 to 1972. His influence lasted for another 19 years but ended, whimpering, in the 1991 Social Credit election campaign.

Like many other leaders, Bennett persevered through years of political failure and scorn. He was born in New Brunswick in 1901 and moved to Kelowna in 1930 as a young married man with children. He was a Conservative, and the successful hardware merchant believed in the values of hardwork and thrift and in the word of the Bible. For celebrations he preferred Ovaltine, and for reading material he chose long columns of figures.

Bennett ruled by the force of his personality. He was a brilliant

Premier W. A. C. Bennett, well ahead of most other provincial politicians as usual, devised a scheme that transferred the provincial debt to provincial agencies. Victoria guaranteed the bonds, but for bookkeeping purposes the province was debt-free. In 1959, in a fairground-style ceremony on Okanagan Lake, the premier fired a burning arrow into a barge carrying the cancelled provincial bonds, though allegedly the fire was set by a hidden RCMP officer. No matter: most voters believed Bennett had made the province debt-free, and few realized the debt was just hidden.

salesman and could create instant visions to dazzle his colleagues and the voters. Since he had no real political ideology, he could switch easily from policy to policy without a tremor. He had switched from the federal to the provincial Conservatives twice before he joined the British Columbia Social Credit party, then an offshoot of the Alberta party run by Premier Ernest Manning, early in 1952.

The appeal of Social Credit had spread over the Rockies when Premier William "Bible Bill" Aberhart defied the political and media establishment during the late 1930s. His kind of religious populism appealed to those in B.C. who mistrusted the polished politicians who ran Canada. Social Credit was strong enough in 1937 to run 18 candidates in the provincial election, but won no seats.

The years since the war had been prosperous times for British Columbia as the damage caused by the war in Europe was repaired and the hungry and homeless were fed and housed, but there were no riches in the political purse.

The Liberal-Conservative coalition, mostly peopled by mediocrities united only by an almost paranoid fear of the CCF, squabbled and offered little leadership or example. When they introduced, just before the July 1952 election, a complicated multiple-choice voting system designed to ensure that the socialists did not slip into power by dividing the free-enterprise vote, they delivered their own death blow. The new system took the antisocialist vote and applied it to make the Socreds — not the Liberals or Conservatives — the winners. The upstarts won 19 seats to the CCF's 18, in a 48-seat house.

Bennett's political luck had eluded him for 20 years but now lodged firmly on his shoulder. He took power on August 1, 1952, at a time of powerful growth and increased federal interest in the provinces. Investment was pouring into the province for pipelines, factories, refineries, lumber and pulp mills. Pay packets were full. Government revenues increased and there was plenty of money to build highways, bridges and create even more jobs. True, many of these projects had been started by Byron "Boss" Johnson, the Coalition leader, but Bennett gaily took the credit.

He quickly tidied up the hospital insurance scheme that had been bungled by the Coalition, got his political friends Robert Bonner and Einar Gunderson into the House — they had not even run in the election — and brought in a "pay-as-you-go" budget. Then he engineered a defeat in the House so that he could call an election and get a working majority. This he did on June 12, 1953, getting 28 seats to the CCF's 14. When the cumbersome counting process was over, the Socreds' popular vote was close to 46 percent.

Bennett now saw a clear road ahead and began to show investors, businessmen and the public that he could run an exciting government, pleasing to almost everyone in the province. A massive roads and highways program, presided over by the eccentric highways minister, Phil Gaglardi, pushed blacktop through the province. The Pacific Great Eastern railway was extended north; bridges, tunnels and schools were built. At last, the Interior was getting attention and development.

There were triumphs — the new Empire Stadium was built in 1954 for the British Empire Games and Roger Bannister's record mile; and there were disasters — the Second Narrows Bridge (now

A ferry plies B.C. waters, but in July 1958, a strike stopped service between the mainland and Vancouver Island. Premier W. A. C. Bennett asked Ottawa to intervene and talked with the union and employers, without success, so the province used the Civil Defence Act to run the private ferries with the strikers as crew. Now Bennett had learned enough about ferries: he offered to provide docks and approach roads if the ferry companies improved service. They refused. In 1959 the province let contracts for two new ferries, the Queen of Tsawwassen *and the* Queen of Sidney, *and built docks at Swartz Bay and Tsawwassen for the start of its own new service in June 1960. About a year later Bennett bought out rival Black Ball for $6.8 million and the* CPR *ended its ferry service. B.C. Ferry Corporation now ran all ferries from the mainland to Victoria, Nanaimo and the Sunshine Coast.*

the Ironworkers' Memorial Second Narrows Crossing) collapsed while it was being built and took 18 workers to their death in Burrard Inlet.

Empire Stadium became the home of the B.C. Lions football team, who joined the Vancouver Mounties baseball team as professional sport was revived. Later, the Vancouver Canucks and Vancouver Blazers were to please and irritate hockey fans.

Bennett, ever the magician with figures, designed an ingenious financial scheme that in effect transferred parts of the provincial debt to corporations running schools, bridges and roads. He then claimed to have lifted the burden of debt from the province.

From the middle 1950s, Premier Bennett soared from success to success in the eyes of the public. Not even a bribery scandal caused by the conduct of Forestry Minister Robert Sommers left any stain. In the 1956 election, under a restored simple majority system, he won 46 percent of the vote.

Within two years, however, Bennett's blue skies were clouding over. Strikes, shutdowns and protests cast doubts on the Bennett magic. And so, on February 12, 1957, the Socreds unveiled a development plan that would dwarf all others. Swedish industrialist Axel Wenner Gren, with a murky reputation during the war and a very

A happy Premier W. A. C. Bennett and worried Prime Minister Lester Pearson flank U.S. President Lyndon Johnson on their way to the Peace Arch to celebrate the Columbia Power Agreement on September 16, 1964. Under the agreement, devised by Bennett to thwart Ottawa, Johnson gave Bennett a cheque for $273,291,661.25 for downstream benefits and flood control.

bad track record in fulfilling promises, had agreed to develop the Peace River Trench, which stretched for hundreds of kilometres in the northern Interior. A monorail would connect pulp mills, towns, power stations, colleges and all the apparatus of a modern industrial state. In return, Wenner Gren got a monopoly in development in the area, about one-tenth of the province.

But Wenner Gren's plans stayed on the drawing table, and Bennett looked for new ways to keep the adrenalin flowing in the province. Ottawa had been arguing with the U.S. for years about how to develop the power locked up in the Columbia River. Now Bennett, never one to let slip a chance of embarrassing Ottawa, trumpeted his vision of Peace River power. Giant dams and an immense artificial lake would provide cheap power to the Lower Mainland and transform northern B.C.

After some fast financial footwork, Bennett declared that

W. A. C. Bennett's plans transform the Interior. The Pacific Great Eastern (later B.C. Rail) connects the towns and villages — and the mills, mines, gas wells and factories — of the north with the Lower Mainland. Hydro dams are built on the Columbia and Peace rivers to provide the power for industrial growth.

Columbia dams: Duncan, built in 1967, is 130 ft. high with a 28-mile-long reservoir; Keenleyside, built in 1968, is 170 ft. high with a 145-mile-long reservoir; Mica, built in 1973, is 800 ft. high with a 16-mile-long reservoir.

Peace dams: Bennett, built in 1967, is 600 ft. high with a 410,000-acre reservoir; Peace Canyon, built in 1980, is 70 ft. high with a 14-mile-long reservoir.

British Columbia was debt-free and on August 2, 1959, in a ceremony suited more to the circus than to politics, he tried to shoot a flaming arrow into a raft carrying the government's cancelled bonds. A concealed Mountie, closer to the target and a better shot, actually started the blaze. The indirect debt, guaranteed by the government, was still there. And when unions shut down the private ferry service between Vancouver Island and the mainland, the premier in a master stroke decided that the government would take over the service.

After the 1960 election, in which the Social Credit vote went down to 39 percent and the CCF's rose to 33, the premier turned his attention to the problems of power from the Peace and Columbia Rivers. In the next three years, the merchant from Kelowna outplayed Prime Minister John Diefenbaker and Justice Minister Davie Fulton, the ranking B.C. Tory. They mishandled

In 1963 Premier W. A. C. Bennett asked Dr. Gordon Shrum to build a university to serve the Fraser Valley. In 1964 the trees on Burnaby Mountain were cut down and roads built through the bush. A year later, Simon Fraser University, designed by Arthur Erickson and Geoffrey Massey and seen here from the air, was open.

the three-way Columbia power negotiations with the United States and Victoria, and Bennett got the terms he wanted. His critics claimed these were the terms the Americans wanted, too.

When privately owned B.C. Electric Railway Company balked at joining the premier's Peace River plan, he took over the company and merged it with the B.C. Power Commission. In the next three years, Bennett happily watched workers build the Peace River dam and Columbia dams. Parties, ceremonies, more bond-burning — these were the days for Bennett to enjoy. In the September 1966 election his popular vote was close to 46 percent.

These were also the days to enjoy for young people and the cultural community. Mostly led by university students, young women and men gloried in a new-found sexual, social, political and artistic freedom. Local poets, writers and artists gained support and, at last, audiences. The Vancouver International Festival attracted actors, singers and audiences from all over the world. In the print media, too, excellence was winning, for these were soon

Coal Mines
Metal Mines

Golden Bear

Snip

S.B. Project

Premier

Bell

Bullmoose
Quintette

Equity
Endako

Gibraltar

Island Copper

Samatosum
Goldstream

Highland Valley

Line
Creek

Pacific
Ocean

Quinsam
Nickel
Plate
Fording
Greenhills

Myra Falls
Similco
Sullivan
Balmer

Byron Creek

to be the times of Allan Fotheringham, Marjorie Nichols, Stuart Keate, Paul St. Pierre and others.

But the boom was levelling off, and the Socreds' well-paid helpers were getting a little greedy and tarnishing the image of probity. Highways Minister Gaglardi, for example, was accused of helping his sons and friends to profit from government contracts and inside information. Gaglardi resigned, but had done little wrong in Bennett's eyes. For the 1969 election the usual kinds of tidbits were offered to voters. Money was plentiful and few parts of the province could claim they had been forgotten. The Socreds drew their highest ever popular vote, close to 47 percent.

But now the once proud Bennett caravan was slowing down. The great achievements that had transformed the face of the province were all in place — huge dams, kilometres of blacktop, including new arterial highways and bridges, a first-rate ferry system, B.C. Hydro, new universities to take advantage of Ottawa's support for higher education. Yet the foundation was rotten. Bennett's bravado and political brilliance had faded. Many of his ministers were incompetent clowns who sought confrontation with teachers, doctors, the poor and the unions. Bennett's total control over the Legislature, with no question period, no real *Hansard* and no desire to share power with the MLAs, even of his own party, now seemed to be petty and malign instead of bold and purposeful. The real costs of the two-rivers policy, with its massive spending and agreements with the Americans, were exposed, and the premier's crude attacks on Ottawa were disturbing even the government's friends.

On August 30, 1972, after a weak election campaign against a bouncy new New Democratic Party leader, Dave Barrett, Bennett's Social Credit party was defeated. Its share of the popular vote sank from 47 to 31 percent and its seats from 38 to 10. The NDP seized 38 seats, with 40 percent of the vote. When W. A. C. Bennett left office on September 13, 1972, he was driven away in a Cadillac by a chauffeur. When Dave Barrett took over, he arrived at Government House in a slightly soiled Volvo. The public was ready for change.

It would be nice to report that British Columbia's left-of-centre politicians, who had been fighting to gain power for more than 40 years, seized their chances when they took over. But only a loyal NDP member would claim success. The Bennett regime had created the infrastructure for a highly industrialized province, and the bigger industries — particularly forestry and mining — had benefited from the improvements in transport and power supply. In 20 years of Socred rule, electrical power generation increased sixfold. The construction industry had grown fat as roads, railways, plants and

A jaunty Dave Barrett gets good news as his staff look on. Barrett celebrated his electoral victory over the tired Socreds in 1972 by driving up to the Legislature in a scruffy Volvo. He broke the hold of right-wing parties in B.C. — but not for long.

docks (the Roberts Bank coal port, for example) were built. The trend to bigger firms, integrated both locally and internationally, continued. New universities and colleges sprouted throughout the province. In short, material prosperity was at hand.

Now the NDP, led by a Jewish, Roman Catholic-educated social worker, very sensible of the diversity of the province and the need for reform, had its chance. It could use the power of the state to improve the quality of life in the province, as Bennett and his businessmen friends had improved its infrastructural assets, and in many areas that happened.

The delivery and generosity of social welfare programs were

improved immensely when a system of 23 community resource boards was set up. An urban transit system, years overdue, began to serve the suburbs and neighbouring municipalities. Provincial car insurance and Agricultural Land Reserve Legislation to curb urban sprawl and protect farmland were introduced in 1973. New wilderness parks were created.

Farmers got an income assurance plan, and provincial government workers got the right to strike. Taxes were increased for mining companies in 1974, and a number of Crown corporations — designed to handle failing forest companies and develop other industries — were formed.

As if to make up for the years out of power, Barrett made Bennett's race to change the province seem a dawdle. The legislation enabling these and other changes was pushed swiftly through the House. In the first year of his government, Barrett introduced 300 important bills into the Legislature, compared with an average of 40 in Bennett's days. And, to show what he was doing, he dragged the Legislature into the modern age by starting a question period and a *Hansard*.

But there was a problem: the NDP tried to bring about a sophisticated, left-of-centre, Scandinavian-style state with the antiquated bureaucractic and parliamentary system bequeathed it by Bennett. There was no adequate committee structure, and caucus meetings were just friendly get-togethers. Instead of cabinet being the place where government priorities were discussed and decided, it was an arena in which some of the ministers diverted parliamentary and financial resources to their own pet projects.

Premier Bennett had been the mainspring of most of his government's operations and, through his financial expertise and conspiratorial techniques, could both direct operations and sense when anything was off course. His staffing needs were small.

Premier Barrett, however, was the leader of a cabinet with members who quickly recognized that a good personal bureaucracy was the foundation of success in Cabinet. Those members who made the best presentations received the resources. This distorted the

government's priorities and meant that good budgeting was almost impossible to achieve, and this in a time of limited economic growth. Barrett, who should have had the staff (and the ability) to control the robber barons and their plans, had neither until the arrival of Marc Eliesen from the NDP in Ottawa. By then it was probably too late. (Twenty years later Eliesen again was called west, this time to head B.C. Hydro.)

Carrying on the family tradition: W. A. C. Bennett shows sons Bill (left) and Russell how to carry on the family hardware business. Soon after he was defeated in 1972, W. A. C. started to reorganize the Socred party so that Bill could carry on the business of the premier's office.

The perception that Barrett could not control his ministers was heightened by the inability of the NDP to explain and justify its policies. Obviously, question period and *Hansard* were not enough.

Convinced of their own abilities and a little heady with success, the cabinet and Barrett's advisers did not seem to realize that to many businesses and most of the folk in the Interior, they were still "the Red Horde." Superb public relations were essential to calm their fears. Instead, there was insensitivity and a sense of "we are the masters now."

Visitors are ferried to Expo 86, a fair and exhibition built on the shore of Vancouver's False Creek. It was opened by Prince Charles and Princess Diana and offered the usual range of national pavilions, restaurants and amusements. Premier Bill Bennett was dismayed by the apparently slow progress in building, so persuaded the entrepreneur par excellence, Jimmy Pattison, to become the fair's dollar-a-day boss. The theme of Expo 86 was transportation and to spread the goodies beyond Vancouver, the province built the SkyTrain and the Coquihalla Highway. When the fair was over, most of the buildings were demolished and the land was sold for housing.

This meant that after three years, when most governments are usually getting into their stride, the NDP was starting to stumble. For some reason, instead of using the time to prepare a campaign, Barrett decided to call an election for December 11, 1975. His loyal supporters did not desert him, and the NDP held onto its popular vote of 39 percent. But the Socreds, revived under W. A. C. Bennett's son Bill, were helped by Liberal and Conservative voters. They got 49 percent — a return to the figures of W.A.C.

Barrett lost his seat as well as the premier's office, but the whole province was the loser, for Barrett was a witty, compassionate, mercurial man whose leadership seemed to be refreshingly free of the taint of financial scandal. He deserved more than a little help from his friends.

Later allegations in the 1990s about payments to get Barrett a seat in the Legislature, however, and about the role of his finance minister, Dave Stupich, in the "Bingogate" affair, have taken away some of the sheen.

Powerful fathers always cast shadows over their children. Throughout Bill Bennett's political life from 1975 to 1986, he

seemed to carry the burden of comparison with his father wearily and sought both to confirm his heritage and, at the same time, to reject it. He confirmed it by embarking on grand schemes such as B.C. Coal, Expo 86 and the British Columbia Resources Investment Corporation. He rejected it by choosing to lead a team rather than be a one-man show, and to transform the machinery of government — something his father would never have done.

Today the dams, bridges, ferries, highways and universities his father built are powerful memorials to W. A. C.'s energy and political skills. But Bill Bennett's B.C. Place Stadium is home only to the B.C. Lions, tractor pulls and sales shows. B.C. Coal became a billion-dollar black hole, and Expo 86 is now just another piece of real estate owned by a wily financier. BCRIC, Bennett's attempt to bring the wonders of people's capitalism to the masses, is just an unpleasant memory. SkyTrain, the exciting, automated, elevated rapid transit system, is a technical success as it weaves its silent

B.C. Place Stadium under construction. The success of building the covered sports stadium on time and on budget was not matched by its use after the first few years. It opened only for the short football season, tractor pulls and trade shows.

path through the suburbs, but experts still wonder whether the technology has cost too much.

Nearly all these projects — and the less spectacular but essential legislation — were wrapped in a web of confusion, half-truths and the bitter confrontation engendered by Bennett's attempts to curb the unions in difficult economic times. The result was that even the successes seem tainted.

Bill Bennett, who was born on April 14, 1932, owed his start in politics to two people — his father and Grace McCarthy, his father's political daughter. After the 1972 defeat, McCarthy, who had been a favourite cabinet minister since December 1966, and another former cabinet minister, Dan Campbell, tramped the province and kept the spirit of Social Credit alive. In Kelowna, Victoria and Vancouver, Bennett senior cajoled friends and political debtors so that his son became his political heir. Liberal MLAs Pat McGeer, Garde Gardom, Alan Williams and Tory Hugh Curtis left their parties to join the young Bennett. And so did the young Dutch-born mayor of Surrey, a Liberal named William Vander Zalm.

These MLAs would be in Bill Bennett's first cabinet, which in December 1975 set about correcting NDP errors. Hydro, ferry and auto insurance costs were increased, and Vander Zalm, the human resources minister, started to demolish the new social welfare system. Unfortunately, though some of the new Bennett government's moves could be justified, they were accompanied by bullying or sneering statements that undercut their value.

The rest of Bennett's first session did little to show that he could match his father's skills in selling his policies to the voters. True, new legislation, based on a report by UBC's Dr. Peter Pearse, tidied and modernized the government's relations with the forest industry. A tight rein on public-service wage increases and on expenditures in general brought a surplus in the government's financial accounts. But Transport Minister Jack Davis blotted his copybook by defrauding the government in a banal airline ticket scheme; a constituency redistribution plan made the government look foolish as it denied involvement and then had to backpedal.

The 1979 Social Credit election campaign was launched by the premier when he laid out details of his plan to give the public shares in the British Columbia Resources Investment Corporation. Most of the Crown corporations created by the NDP were to be incorporated in the new entity and the people, not the state, were to be the owners, Bennett claimed. With BCRIC as his banner, he won his second election. The NDP was two percentage points (46 to 48) and five seats (26 to 31) behind.

Under Bennett's BCRIC proposal, everyone in B.C. would get five free shares: any Canadian could buy up to 5,000. Soon there were about 10 million free shares in the hands of British Columbians; 80 million extra shares had been bought through banks and dealers — many by people who borrowed to get the cash. BCRIC was listed on the Vancouver Stock Exchange on August 7, 1979, at $6.12 a share, 12 cents above face value. A year later it was selling at about the same price.

Then BCRIC president David Helliwell announced that the corporation would buy a controlling interest in Kaiser Resources at $55 a share. Market experts pointed out that the same deal could have been made a little earlier at $44 a share. The media claimed that a number of people had done very well by buying into Kaiser just before the sale. Another scandal. Another inquiry absolving the principals of wrongdoing, but the damage had been done. Helliwell quit and by May 1981 BCRIC was selling at $5.50; a year later it sold at $2.95. The government removed restrictions on share ownership and made it just another company. It slowly faded away.

In the spring of 1980, the premier had announced some big projects. Vancouver would get a sports stadium the equal of any in North America, an international transportation exposition, a trade centre and a rapid transit system to link them all. As the months passed, a series of land deals, grants from Ottawa, bond issues and other financial arrangements was cobbled together to provide the money. The stadium was rushed ahead and built on budget. Bennett proudly opened it in November 1982 when he switched

The men who negotiated the end of the Bennett-Solidarity struggle: International Woodworkers of America leader Jack Munro (above) and the premier's chief aide and adviser, Norman Spector (following page). Critics of Munro in the labour movement complained, unfairly, that he had been duped by the wily Spector in the talks at Premier Bill Bennett's Kelowna home. Spector went on to become Prime Minister Brian Mulroney's adviser on the Constitution and then ambassador to Israel.

on the fans to blow up the stadium's air-supported fibreglass and Teflon roof.

Next it was B.C. Coal's turn. After years of meetings and rumours, Don Phillips, the minister for economic development, announced that B.C. was going to sign an agreement with the Japanese to supply coal from deposits in the northeast. Eight million tonnes a year for 15 years, it was announced on January 21, 1981, would be dug from the massive opencast pits. Ottawa was going to contribute $100 million worth of work on a coal port at Prince Rupert and on upgrading Canadian National rail links. B.C. would pay for the new railway lines, townsites, highways and power stations. Critics quickly maintained that this infrastructure would cost about $1 billion and that the price to the Japanese was a giveaway. The pits, however, were dug, ports and railways built and families moved into the new towns. Eventually coal was on its way to Japanese smelters. Critics continued to complain about the cost overruns and the creative accounting. Later, the world price of coal had dropped, prices were renegotiated and one of the firms running the pits ran into financial trouble. Years of argument and mediation dulled the lustre of B.C. coal. One cynic said it would have been cheaper to have told the Japanese that if they did the digging themselves they could have the coal free.

The recession of 1981–82 provided the background for Bennett's fight with labour, one that would last for the rest of his time as premier. In February 1982, he told the province that he was setting limits on government expenditures and on raises for civil servants. The latter were asking for raises that averaged 27 percent and, since Bennett offered 6.5, it was obvious that confrontation was near. On April 6, 30,000 civil servants walked out and ferry service stopped. There were talks, rotating walkouts and eventually, on September 20, Bennett and the unions worked out a complex deal that sent everyone back to work. By that time the unemployment rate in B.C. was 14 percent.

Bennett won his third election victory in May 1983 and decided to start an even tougher "restraint" package. The NDP was, in effect, leaderless, as Barrett seemed to have lost interest, and Bob Skelly did not take over as party leader for a year.

In two budgets and 40 separate bills, Bennett's government launched an onslaught on government expenditures and institutions and cut civil-service jobs. On July 27, about 20,000 people demonstrated in front of the Legislature. Guards were posted outside the building and Bennett had a bodyguard.

Labour had to provide most of the political opposition, and Operation Solidarity, involving many B.C. unions and some fringe groups, was formed. A general strike was set for October 31, and between 50,000 and 60,000 people joined a march past the Hotel Vancouver on October 15. The Socreds were inside at their annual convention.

Soon afterward, olive branches became fashionable. Jack Munro, then the International Woodworkers of America leader, met Bennett and his chief adviser, Norman Spector, at Bennett's home in Kelowna. The strike threat was withdrawn; Bennett offered to reconsider some of the measures and to consult union leaders on the

Bill Bennett's "restraint" budget brings out crowds to protest. Twenty thousand people surround the Legislature on July 27, 1983. Bennett has a bodyguard but no one is hurt as Solidarity, a coalition of union members and left-leaning members of the public, becomes the unofficial political opposition.

restraint program. The collapse of Solidarity left bitter tastes in many union mouths. Bennett did little better: in December a poll showed that 60 percent of respondents were dissatisfied with his restraint program and 30 percent satisfied. The resentment and disappointment continued and, although Bennett told his cheering convention supporters in October 1985 that restraint had worked and that civil servants' jobs were safe, he decided to quit politics on May 22, 1986.

The days when the Bennetts and Barrett ruled the province truly fashioned its future. Almost all the troubles that disturb the sleep of politicians, editorialists and thinking citizens in the 2000s — declining resources, growth of environmentalism, First Nations rights, land claims, emphasis on human rights, changes in the Constitution and a growing divide between the Lower Mainland and the Interior — were born or roused from sleep during those 30 or so years.

These issues gathered little coverage in the media and excited little public awareness during this time, for most eyes were on the turbulent provincial world of politics, economics, labour and development, but their effects were massive and long-lasting.

In 1960 Ottawa recognized First Nations people's right to vote (they had received the provincial vote in 1949), and the same year saw the first of two reports by Professor Harry Hawthorn of UBC on the sorry state of Native people both in B.C. and Canada. The second was used as the basis of a federal White Paper that favoured the assimilation of Native people into white Canadian society, an idea rejected by Native leaders. In 1968 agricultural research scientist Len Marchand was picked by Kamloops voters to be the first aboriginal MP. Five years later the Supreme Court affirmed Native ownership of land.

After several years of talking, negotiating and arm-twisting in Canada and Britain, Prime Minister Pierre Trudeau celebrated the patriation of the Constitution in 1982 when Queen Elizabeth arrived to sign the document in Ottawa. Attached to the Constitution was the Charter of Rights, which was to change the lives of both First Nations and other citizens.

Forest firms, running out of trees, especially first growth, eyed the remote areas of the province. When news broke of plans to log Meares Island on the west coast of Vancouver Island, a group formed the Friends of Clayoquot Sound in 1979 to protest in the activist tradition of Greenpeace, the international environmental organization founded in Kitsilano in 1970.

The big projects of the Bennetts may have favoured the resource industries initially, but they hastened the death of farming in the Interior and gave an artificial injection of life to industries that were threatened, if not doomed. In hindsight, money spent on the growing new technology would have made a better bargain, even at the cost of votes. As resources ran out, they took with them the jobs, communities and hope that had kept isolated communities alive. During the 1980s the gap between the buoyant Lower Mainland and the apprehensive, resentful Interior widened. The political climate of 2001 was the result.

We jump to the present and land in the very different world of Douglas Coupland. Writer, designer, sculptor, social commentator and world traveller, he was raised in West Vancouver and educated at the Emily Carr Insitute of Art and Design. These two excerpts are from his book, City of Glass.

Downtown Vancouver in 2000, with the Granville Street Bridge pointing the way. The first inhabitants had many names for the forests, streams and ponds that once covered the area and provided homes for the First Nations and animals who lived here. Now it's all one place — Vancouver — and the only totem poles seen by visitors are in Stanley Park.

The Rest of Canada

Vancouver is not part of Canada. Not really. There's a genuine sense of disconnection from the Rest of Canada that we feel here. While Ontario looms large in the minds of most other Canadians, said province simply doesn't enter our minds from one week to the next.

In looking through the souvenir book from my high school's twentieth-year reunion (Sentinel Class of 1979), I noticed that dozens and dozens of class-mates had married Americans from Washington, Oregon and California, and only a small number had connected in any way to the east. This makes sense; Vancouverites have much in common with West Coast Americans, and at the same time remain highly distinct from them. Americans wonder how Vancouverites can be so cavalier about their link to Canada, so you have to tell them that, every decade or so, votes are held back east to see if the country even plans to stick together.

There's nothing unpatriotic about Vancouver's psychic disconnection from the Rest of Canada — it's a reality fostered by Vancouver's distance from Canada's centre, and from a tradition of abandoning that very centre to try something new. To ignore these factors would be foolish. In a thousand years, Canada won't be the same country it is now, nor will it probably be the same in five hundred, a hundred, fifty or even ten. My own hunch is that Vancouver will eventually evolve into a city state going as far north as Whistler, as far east as the Fraser Canyon and then to the U.S. border. It's okay to daydream about what sort of country Quebec would make if it split away, but to think of Vancouver as separate feels heretical ...

Sto:lo

Vancouver originally had not one, but many names given to it by its first residents, the Sto:lo Nation, but most Vancouverites didn't know this until recently. By the same token, the Queen Charlotte Islands up north are called Haida Gwaii, which makes good sense, as the Haida were the first folks there. I heard somebody on the radio once say, "Who the hell was Queen Charlotte?" Good question — and so Haida Gwaii it is.

Growing up in Vancouver, you end up with a slightly schizoid relationship with First Nations cultures. In elementary school, you colour in totem poles and make Haida-style masks. Years go on, and everywhere you look, Native motifs are splashed about. You're told, "This is your culture, this is part of your heritage." But then you get older and realize that, well, it's actually somebody else's heritage, and you have no claim to it at all. This makes you feel queasy about the time spent thinking it was your own culture. And if First Nations culture isn't part of your heritage, then what should be your relationship with it? Do you respectfully keep your distance? Do you try and get involved? And what are you to make of the crowds who flock to stare at the totem poles at Stanley Park?

Native land rights are probably the biggest issue facing the province of B.C., let alone Vancouver. Unlike the U.S. and other parts of Canada, we have never fought any major wars with the First Nations peoples, nor were there any treaties — land simply got taken, so it's all mucky and undefined. Should this issue come to a head the same week that various Asian scenarios go critical and the Big One hits, Vancouver is going to be one heck of an interesting place to be.

1986 TO 2002

Challenges at Home and Abroad

Bill Bennett's decision to resign after Expo 86 ended the reigns of
the Bennetts and of Barrett, but there was something disturbing
in its implications: it seemed to mark the end of competent government in B.C.

Public life was not as simple as it once was. The foundation of
the province's economy, the resource industries, was under assault
from nature and the growing power of the believers in conservation
and protecting the environment. Land claims and the rights of
First Nations were affecting politics, the courts and industry in

both rural and urban areas. The province's relationship with the rest of Canada became tense, and the growth of a global economy limited the province's power even further.

At a time when excellence was essential, there seemed to be a decline in the competence of the province's leaders. They lacked the skills in administration, politics and leadership needed to run political entities.

It's easy to tag Bill Vander Zalm as a charming wildman, caring little for the niceties of democracy; Mike Harcourt as a meek bumbler led astray by stronger minds; Glen Clark as a strongman determined to succeed, foolishly unwilling to be bound by the usual restraints; and Ujjal Dosanjh as a facile manipulator and caretaker.

But all of them were creatures of their times. Many observers believe that since the 1980s our political, cultural and public lives had "dumbed down." Voters sought easy, pleasant answers to difficult, disturbing questions. Single-issue groups were concerned only with forcing the government to accede to their wishes. The people who provided the services essential to the new society — doctors, lawyers, nurses and others — took full advantage of the lack of leadership and accountability. Most of the media had become passive, waiting to be told, easy to suborn.

Of all the candidates to succeed Bennett in 1986, only four had a reasonable chance — cabinet ministers Grace McCarthy, Brian Smith, Bud Smith and Vander Zalm. Vander Zalm campaigned for the premier's office with his usual effervescence and charm and was well ahead of the others before the leadership convention opened at Whistler in July. At the convention he led all the ballots and was sitting in the premier's office in Victoria on August 6, 1986. He called the election for October 22 and easily beat the NDP's fumbling Bob Skelly (who had succeeded Dave Barrett as leader in May 1984), 47 seats to 22. No other party elected a member. Skelly resigned as leader of the NDP less than a month later.

The new premier had grown up in wartime Holland, where he knew danger, hunger and hardship. He came to Canada with his

Stephen Rogers was one of many ministers in the Vander Zalm government who was accused of political misconduct, and he resigned his cabinet seat. Cleared after an inquiry, he rejoined cabinet and went to England to see how Prime Minister Margaret Thatcher had run her campaign of privatization. Later the government sold B.C. Hydro's gas division and railway to private firms.

It's a rare example of Bill and Lillian Vander Zalm being out of step, but their lack of synchronization didn't halt their confident, successful march to victory at the Socred leadership convention in Whistler in July 1986.

family after the war, worked in the gardening industry and lived and participated in the conservative Christian communities of the Lower Mainland. Vander Zalm prospered, married, raised a family, entered politics and was elected mayor of Surrey. After an unsuccessful bid for Vancouver's city hall, he stepped into Bill Bennett's cabinet and, after Whistler, the premier's office.

The five years of his leadership were, in essence, an exercise in the politics of absurdity. Vander Zalm, relying on his immense charm, paid little attention to his caucus, his cabinet, senior bureaucrats or the code of conduct that generally governs politics in Western countries. He did what he wanted, when he wanted, and lacked the good sense to realize he was failing. Most members of the cabinet and caucus, senior bureaucrats and party officials — the people who normally provide the checks and balances to a wayward political leader — seemed unwilling or unable to act. Those who did protest, by resignation or other means, were marginalized.

The NDP was paralyzed at first by another search for a leader. No one of note seemed eager to take over. Harcourt got the job the next April, but it took him several months to organize his demoralized party. As a result, the opposition to Vander Zalm initially came chiefly from the media (often relying on tips from the new, bright NDP backbenchers) and unions.

Vander Zalm's policies were, like Bill Bennett's, focused on curbing the powers of unions — particularly those in the public service — and on making business feel at home.

In the 1987 Throne Speech the government said it would reduce the deficit and restore business confidence, and a task force would select Crown corporations that could be sold to private business. To learn how to do the trick, Vander Zalm sent Stephen Rogers, businessman and environment minister, to England to talk to officials directing Prime Minister Margaret Thatcher's privatization program. A week later the B.C. budget showed how the deficit was to be cut: personal income tax and sales taxes were going up. On the expenditure side, welfare payments would be increased.

On April 30, Vander Zalm flew to Ottawa for talks on the Constitution.

When Prime Minister Pierre Trudeau brought the Constitution home from Westminster in 1982 and then attached the Charter of Rights, British Columbians were interested but not concerned. They gradually realized that patriation and the Charter changed

It's a typical blustery, bitterly cold day in northern British Columbia as Rick Hansen pumps his wheelchair on the highway outside Prince George in March 1987. Hansen was nearing the end of his worldwide "Man in Motion" tour to raise funds for and awareness of research into spinal injuries. Seven years earlier, another British Columbian, Terry Fox, had crossed Canada to raise funds for cancer research after losing part of one leg to cancer. He had to end his tour early and was brought home, where he died at age 22.

much of public life, as did the provincial response to the so-called Meech Lake Accord of 1987 and the Charlottetown Accord of 1991. The signing of the Free Trade Agreement with the United States showed that B.C.'s prosperity, always vulnerable because of its dependence on resources for export, could be in even more danger.

When the Queen came to Ottawa to sign the new Constitution in 1982, Trudeau had reached the summit of his achievements. The Constitution recognized existing treaties with aboriginals, a matter of some concern to British Columbians just facing up to the problem of land claims. Their provincial governments, shortsightedly, had regarded the claims as mostly a matter for Ottawa, which had taken responsibility for First Nations in the 1871 Confederation agreement. They would soon realize, however, that the claims were their problem, too.

Tacked onto the Constitution was the second part of Trudeau's triumph, a Canadian Charter of Rights. This would affect relations with First Nations, the courts, police work, social life and the workplace.

The Meech Lake Accord was an attempt by Conservative Prime Minister Brian Mulroney to bring Quebec into the constitutional fold. (Some late-night stickhandling by Trudeau, in a bid to get agreement on the Constitution five years earlier, was seen by Quebec as foul play, and Premier Rene Levesque had refused to join the game.)

Norman Spector, who had been Premier Bill Bennett's chief adviser, was now working for Mulroney as secretary to the cabinet for federal-provincial relations. He helped design a plan that would declare Quebec a "distinct society." To persuade the other premiers to accept this concession to Quebec, many of Ottawa's powers (among them immigration, appointment of Supreme Court judges and opting out of programs) were to be handed over to the provinces. The premiers, including Vander Zalm, went home to get the deal approved by their legislatures. No majority — all would have to agree.

Trudeau scorned the accord and called the premiers "snivellers." Elijah Harper, a First Nations member of the Manitoba Legislature, refused assent to debate the agreement and so gave Manitoba a chance to get out of the accord. Newly elected Premier Clyde Wells withdrew the accord from debate in Newfoundland's House of Assembly. Meech was doomed.

Four years later Joe Clark, appointed constitutional affairs minister by Mulroney and still a faithful supporter of the man who had stolen the Conservative leadership from him, tried to cobble a new constitutional deal together and called a series of meetings with the premiers. Quebec was to be offered a larger set of powers and a guarantee of a quarter of the seats in the Commons, even if the province's population fell. Bigger bites of the federal pie were offered to the premiers (Mike Harcourt now represented B.C. in place of Bill Vander Zalm) and First Nations were to get increased power.

Julie Belmas was one of a group of activists dubbed the Squamish Five, whose targets included B.C.'s power lines. The group was broken up by the RCMP and imprisoned. Belmas, the most articulate of the group, applied for parole in 1988. Premier Bill Vander Zalm contacted the parole board and was accused of improperly trying to influence the board's decision; an inquiry later cleared him. Belmas was freed.

This time the provincial legislatures would not be given the final word: Canadians would vote on the Charlottetown Accord, riding by riding, in a national referendum on October 26, 1992. The national media, academics, business leaders and politicians of all stripes urged Canadians to vote "yes." Only a few brave souls stood firm.

When the voting was over, the "nays" had won. In B.C. more than 67 percent voted against — the highest in Canada. Constitutional reform was tucked away. The Tories were demolished in the next federal election.

B.C.'s reaction to Meech and Charlottetown showed that distrust of and resentment against central Canada were still powerful forces. Later these sentiments helped the Alberta-born Reform and Canadian Alliance parties gain a grip on B.C.'s federal seats. (The Reform party, with Preston Manning as leader, was founded in Winnipeg in 1987 while Meech was in process.)

It would be nice to think the people of B.C. were worried about a potential breakup of their nation into a set of weak minor fiefdoms, led by politicians whose competence and honesty were often even more suspect than those of their federal rivals, but Senator Pat Carney was probably right when she selected concessions to Quebec and to First Nations as the reasons for B.C.'s rejection.

The Free Trade Agreement (the abolition of tariffs and promotion of greater movement of goods and services between Canada and the U.S.) had not been one of Prime Minister Mulroney's election promises in 1984, and the appropriate research into the costs and benefits for Canada started in Ottawa, well after the talks with the United States had begun. But after his first meeting with President Ronald Reagan and their concert rendering of "When Irish Eyes Are Smiling" in Quebec City, Mulroney pressed on relentlessly, changing his negotiators like a hockey coach, until an agreement was reached in September 1987, just before the deadline imposed by the American "fast-track" procedure.

For a while the agreement meant little to most British Columbians. They still had to pay duties and taxes on their return from shopping in the United States. Later, most of the duties were phased out — but the taxes remained. For business people there were many ramifications: now they had to regard the U.S. as both a market to be exploited and a source of powerful competition.

The agreement was supposed to mean the end of simple trade

*T*he province's fishery was started by First Nations thousands of years ago but was gradually taken over by non-Native people who persuaded the government to restrict aboriginal fishing. Local fishermen were joined by immigrants such as the Japanese and, after the 1939–45 war, by multinational firms from North America, Europe and Asia operating fleets of boats and factory ships.

Like the forests, the province's seas and rivers provided much to humans, but this abundance was foolishly exploited, a fact admitted by industry and government only when stocks fell low. Fishboat owners were bought out by government as the industry dwindled. In 1998 selective fishing began: some species were off limits until they recovered.

Fishers were not the only ones to blame: industrialization, the growth of cities and global warming were affecting the ocean. Some brave souls, however, believed that new attitudes, better research and management and changes in the climate would bring back some of the fish.

disputes, but even while the negotiations were going on in Washington and Ottawa, softwood lumber producers in the western states were complaining that low provincial stumpage rates (cutting fees) were a subsidy. There was a lot of talk and posturing (Premier Vander Zalm blundered into the debate at one stage), but eventually Canada agreed to impose a 15 percent export tax. This avoided a countervailing duty threatened by the Americans and kept the money in Canada.

The debate about the value of free trade continued long after the signing of the FTA. The softwood lumber agreement was the centre of a renewed trade squabble in 2001. Was water included? Health care services? And what were the implications of including Mexico to make the pact the North American Free Trade Agreement?

Rita Johnston (left) and Grace McCarthy stride out of the Legislature. Friends for a while, they became political rivals when Premier Bill Vander Zalm resigned. Foolishly and callously, the party picked Johnston as leader. McCarthy's claim to the leadership, based on talent and her work in saving the party after W. A. C. Bennett's defeat, was rejected.

In June 1987, the unions in B.C. called a general strike. About 250,000 members stopped work to protest Socred labour legislation that had set up a public-sector pay commission with powers over wage awards.

Next on deck: Vander Zalm's plan for decentralization of government. Eight regions, each led by a minister of state, would bring government closer to the people, he claimed. But the difficulties soon sapped the government's enthusiasm and the plan withered away. Still, Vander Zalm's plans to cut government began in earnest on October 3, when he announced that $3 billion worth of provincially owned assets would be sold to private firms. B.C. Hydro's gas division was sold to Inland Natural Gas, and Hydro's railway went to an American company; B.C. Systems Corporation and highways maintenance contracts were also sold.

The Liberal party, after a long hibernation, came to life. It had no sitting members but much ambition and elected Gordon Wilson as leader. Vander Zalm, however, was slipping into a trap. His formidable charm was losing its power and his problems were becoming more complex. Naturally, now he listened more to the people he had hired, professional and expert, and less to members who were not so sophisticated and had their own agendas. The Socred caucus complained often, but not too loudly. Some members quit.

By-election results are difficult to interpret well, but most experts agreed that Bill Barlee's win for the NDP in Boundary-Similkameen in May 1988 was a warning sign; the riding had been held by the Socreds for 22 years. In time, more by-elections would be lost and two cabinet ministers would resign.

Vander Zalm continued selling provincial property. A Hong Kong financier, Li Ka-Shing, bought some of the land used for Expo 86 in Vancouver in a complicated deal worth, experts estimated, $500 million. Peter Toigo, a B.C. entrepreneur and friend of the premier, was interested in the land, too, and critics claimed that Vander Zalm tried to influence the decision.

In July 1988, just less than two years into his mandate, the premier lost two of his cabinet, Grace McCarthy and Brian

Smith. Both had served in Bill Bennett's cabinet and both had run for the Social Credit leadership. McCarthy complained of the arrogance of "non-elected officials." Soon afterward, Vander Zalm announced that adviser David Poole's responsibilities would be reduced.

The premier's inability to separate his actions as premier from his private beliefs was shown in August, when the government admitted paying investigators to spy on a pro-choice group. On another occasion, emboldened by his conservative Christian supporters, he tried to enter the debate about abortions by questioning their financing under Medicare.

The premier solidified his hold on the religious communities when the rules governing provincial assistance to private schools were revised in 1989. Once the term "private school" usually meant an imitation of an upper-class English institution; now, many pri-

*A*s the province moved away from producing goods and toward producing ideas and services, the government had to improve and put more resources into education. Finding the money would be difficult. By 2001 schools cost nearly $5 billion a year; higher education (universities, colleges and institutes) close to $2 billion; total: about one-quarter of the province's money. And money wasn't the only problem.

Disputes about strikes and bargaining in education drew attention during the 2001 election. Crucial issues included accountability of teachers, control of material and techniques used in classrooms, program choices for parents and help for disabled children.

The Liberals had promised to give school boards more power, but devolution doesn't always stop conveniently. Would "charter schools," funded by government but managed by parents and teachers and independent of any school board, be on the way?

Universities were facing pressure to industrialize, to make their learning more closely tied to employment and even to let industry provide and control some of the teaching. And the growth of global communication meant select teachers from anywhere in the world could provide education to the most remote campus. These developments would be highly controversial and could be dangerous for academic freedom.

Bud Smith, a Social Credit cabinet minister under Bill Bennett and Bill Vander Zalm, photographed in 1986. His career path was not smooth. Perhaps his greatest trouble came after Bill Reid, former auto dealer then Socred cabinet minister, was accused of mishandling lottery funds. The RCMP wanted to charge Reid, but Smith, then attorney general, refused. NDP opposition member Moe Sihota hired a lawyer to conduct a private inquiry, and Smith made derogatory comments about the lawyer on a cellular phone; the calls were over-heard and taped and Smith was accused of trying to obstruct justice. He resigned, but was cleared later.

vate schools were controlled by religious groups. Under the new rules, Victoria would pay 50 per cent of their costs, with churches and parents making up the difference with fees, bingo games and other fundraising, but the schools had to teach the basic provincial curriculum and then fit in religious and other studies.

The start of August 1988 brought another blow for Vander Zalm. David Poole, his adviser and, said some, his eminence grise, resigned.

Despite high interest rates (the bank rate in early 1989 was 12.12 percent), the Socreds balanced their next budget and promised to add 15,000 university seats. But after the summer the troubles began again. Another so-called safe Socred seat in the Interior (Cariboo) was won by the NDP, and the seamy side of the Social Credit movement was dragged into the light when Bill Reid, the tourism minister, had to resign; more than $250,000 in lottery grants controlled by his ministry had been handed to a firm con-trolled by Reid's campaign manager. An investigation later showed that it had not even applied for a grant.

The media, some supporters and lots of voters may have found

Vander Zalm less than perfect, but the party faithful at a rally in Vancouver at the end of October did not agree. He was greeted with long cheers, those opposed to abortion had a tame audience, and there were even some racist sentiments aired to show that the Old Guard was still on duty. Two weeks later, however, came the sixth straight by-election loss. Elizabeth Cull, soon to be an NDP cabinet minister, won Brian Smith's old seat in Oak Bay. To add to the gloom, federal polls showed the NDP ahead of both the ruling Tories and Opposition Liberals.

The Socreds' 1990 budget was balanced, but Vander Zalm's political world was going topsy-turvy. On July 12, Attorney General Bud Smith quit in the wake of the Bill Reid scandal.

A logging truck leaves the Carmanah Valley on Vancouver Island. The valley, with its stand of more than 200 rare giant Sitka spruce, became a symbol of environmental conflict in B.C.

Deputy attorney general Ted Hughes led an inquiry into Smith's conduct. Smith was cleared and returned to cabinet.

Worse was to come: Vander Zalm owned a controversial theme park called Fantasy Garden World just off Highway 99 in Richmond. As his troubles grew, the management of the park and that of the government became irrevocably tangled, and he tried to sell the park. When he was questioned by the Opposition and the media, he told them that his wife, Lillian, was in charge. But documents showed that the premier, not his wife, owned and managed Fantasy Garden World.

In September 1990, Vander Zalm sold the park to a Taiwanese firm for $14.5 million, but the sale did not lighten his load. On February 13, 1991, in a civil suit against real estate-agent Faye Leung, it was alleged that the premier had offered to split the commission on the Fantasy Garden World sale and that his wife had told the Taiwanese firm her husband could help it set up a bank in Canada. There was also a mysterious cheque for $20,000 which, it was alleged, was given to Ms. Leung in a hotel room late at night for safekeeping.

The premier announced that he had asked Ted Hughes, now conflict-of-interest commissioner, to inquire into the accusations, but it was the last flicker of life: after more charges that he had lied to the Legislature, Vander Zalm received Hughes' report. The premier resigned on April 2.

In September he was charged with breach of trust. He was acquitted, but the court said he was foolish to mix public and private business.

Now came the Socreds' chance to show that Vander Zalm's reign was an aberration. A new, unsullied leader, with no ties to the former premier, would show that the party had cast off the trappings of nonsense and deceit. But delegates at the leadership convention in July chose Vander Zalm's long-term ally, Rita Johnston, and she became premier.

On October 17, after a campaign riddled with errors and confusion, the Social Credit party was cut to seven seats. The NDP led

by Mike Harcourt took over, and the Liberals under new leader, Gordon Wilson, became the Opposition.

Could any government be worse than Bill Vander Zalm's? After 10 years of the NDP's Mike Harcourt, Glen Clark and Ujjal Dosanjh, the media and voters in 2001 answered "yes."

Critics claimed that the NDP governments were responsible for a series of foolish, perhaps criminal, misdeeds. And they used the tags "Bingogate," "Ferrygate," "Budgetgate," "Casinogate" and "Carriergate" to describe them. The absurdity of equating Watergate, a scandal that brought down a U.S. president, with, say, the mismanagement of a provincial ferry-building program, seems to have eluded many of the critics and protesters.

Historians may see these affairs as eddies in the flow of British Columbia's political and economic life, but they diverted attention from important issues such as the downturn of the economy and the shrinking of the once great engines of local economic growth, forestry, fishing and mining. How severe was the impact

Mike Harcourt celebrates his win over Bill Vander Zalm's short-term successor, Premier Rita Johnston, in November 1991. After life under Vander Zalm the people of British Columbia looked forward to happier, calmer days under the modest, virtuous former mayor of Vancouver. Little did they know what tumult lay ahead.

The clothes suit the wearers: colourful, charismatic Judy Tyabji and her earnest, prosaic husband, Gordon Wilson, an NDP cabinet minister, are on their way to a dinner in Wilson's honour in spring of 1999. Their romance was once the talk of the town and his political future seemed bright, but defeat and obscurity loomed.

of environmentalism, of land claims and assertion of the rights of First Nations? There were demands for medical care for all who wanted it, and high-quality education would be required for the new economy.

Forgotten, too, was the need to find out how many of B.C.'s difficulties had external causes. It was one province in a federal state where considerable power resided in the national government. And Canada was a small state with limited power.

With high hopes, Mike Harcourt spent his first day as premier of an NDP government in Victoria on November 5, 1991. The new premier, as ordinary as Vander Zalm was unusual, had graduated as a lawyer in 1968, joined the NDP and was elected a Vancouver alderman in 1972.

Next step up: mayor of Vancouver, a position Harcourt filled for four terms from 1980 until he was elected an MLA in 1986. Nothing, it seemed, could stop him and in 1987 he was acclaimed leader of the NDP. In November, he defeated Johnston, and when he presided over his first cabinet meeting in Victoria, there were around the table some faces voters would come to know well — Glen Clark, Dan Miller, Elizabeth Cull and Moe Sihota.

In March 1992, Harcourt greeted the Legislature and promised accountable leadership, freedom of information and first steps toward recognition of aboriginal title and self-government. The Freedom of Information Bill was introduced five days later, its provisions to go into effect over 18 months. A favourable vote in a referendum led to a recall law.

Harcourt's finance minister was Glen Clark, whose first budget was a pleasant surprise for conservative critics: the province's economic growth was the best in Canada, yet Clark cut spending.

But he became a villain when he introduced his second budget in 1993. It included a surtax on the owners of homes worth more than $500,000. The shouts of protest from Vancouver's west side and the North Shore could be heard across the water in Victoria. Harcourt stepped in and moved Clark to the employment portfolio. It was a familiar tale in the new B.C. politics: a proposal is greeted by an outburst of rage, gleefully reported and encouraged by the media. The government makes little or no attempt to justify or improve the proposal and turns tail.

The workaday world of provincial policies was briefly put aside when British Columbians read about a romance between Liberal leader Gordon Wilson and the House Leader, Judy Tyabji. Both were married to others; both had children. A letter from Tyabji to Wilson was leaked to the media. The romance cost both their jobs, for in September the Liberals picked Gordon Campbell as their leader and gave the lovers the heave-ho. Campbell, a developer and former mayor of Vancouver, was more to the taste of the conservative faction of the party and its prosperous backers.

Wilson and Tyabji, who married later, formed the Progressive Democratic Alliance, and Wilson became its first leader. Still later, in a move that showed the flexibility of political loyalty in B.C., he joined the NDP and served as cabinet minister.

Who steps in when there's no official Opposition in the Legislature? Experts offered these suggestions:

1. **The media**. Their talent, determination and expertise arguably were strongest when the Bennetts and Dave Barrett were in power. Some reporters and columnists have extended that excellence into the new century, but overall there has been a steady reduction in expertise and in the space, time and money allotted to political coverage since the mid-1980s. The result has often been lazy acceptance of claims or statements that needed examination. The takeover of local media by conglomerates may well introduce at best more blandness or, at worst, all-out support of a purely business agenda.

2. **The New Democrat Party**. Not confined to the Legislature, with labour support it might mount some opposition. Gaining and keeping the public's trust, attention and affection with new leaders and new policies would be the problem.

3. **The Green Party**. With few debts to labour, a personable leader and experience in swaying public opinion, it could be more successful if its component parts could stay together.

4. **Special interest groups and genuine political commentators**. Using meetings, small magazines and the internet, these could weave a web of opposition, but the multiplicity of voices would be a problem.

Modern B.C. was created by megaprojects, but soon after Harcourt took power Alcan, the aluminium firm and creator of Kitimat, launched a project that would show that many British Columbians were no longer mesmerized by giant projects. Rather, they were worried that the province's bountiful resources were in danger and dwindling.

Alcan wanted to increase its Kitimat aluminum plant's capacity by damming and diverting most of the water in the Nechako River, already diverted to feed power to Alcan. The plan, kept secret at first, was attacked by environmentalists, First Nations, sport fishers, the commercial fishers' union, nature lovers and some commentators. They pointed out that the diversion to provide water for another power plant could, among other things, destroy the Stuart River sockeye run.

At first the government did nothing, for the Alcan proposal was based on a 1948 agreement. The diversion would do more good than harm, the protesters were told. But as work on the diversion went on, opposition grew. Alcan claimed it had already spent $500 million on the project. The government started bargaining with the company, offering more power from B.C. Hydro, money and other inducements. Negotiations dragged on, with threats from both the government and Alcan, but an agreement was reached in August 1997. Protesters, however, claimed the government had not protected the Nechako and that the river's flow was still restricted.

Like most large ports, Vancouver once sheltered a shipbuilding industry. Wars, peace, the Depression and economic booms and slumps had brought good and bad times, and by the 1990s the end was clearly near. Yards on the North Shore and on Vancouver Island were mostly rusting hulks, and many skilled union workers were on pogey or busy in other jobs. In 1994 Harcourt announced a 10-year plan to revive the industry. As part of the plan, local yards would build three new high-speed catamaran ferries for B.C. Ferries' Horseshoe Bay-to-Nanaimo run.

The fast-ferry plan seemed a good idea — if you didn't look

Moe Sihota, scourge in Opposition and difficult colleague in government, is seen here after rejoining the NDP cabinet in 1998. He had stepped down after facing charges that he had helped friend Herb Dhaliwal, a federal Liberal cabinet minister, get a taxi licence for a firm in which he had an interest. It was Sihota's second departure from cabinet. In 2002 he was a television host.

too carefully. Tourism was a growing industry and the provincial ferry fleet would eventually need new ships. Local shipyards were mostly dark and silent. Why not retrain the workers in new ship-building technology and let them build some high-speed catamarans? That was the dream.

But there was no immediate need for new ferries. The design was faulty: the vessels were under-powered; their hulls caused too-big waves at high speed; they could not handle enough vehicles; they could not be refuelled from onboard tankers while running, as could the standard ferries. The catamarans' route was not suitable for high-speed travel. The business plan was flawed, and the process of planning, design and manufacture was hurried, with

Brian Smith, B.C. Hydro boss, listens to questions at a press conference during Premier Glen Clark's first crisis, in the spring of 1996. Hydro chiefs John Laxton and John Sheehan and some well-known NDP members were accused of profiting from a Hydro contract for a power development in Pakistan. Clark appointed Smith, once a Socred cabinet minister, and later Prime Minister Brian Mulroney's man in charge of CN Rail, to run Hydro.

little time for consultation. When experts warned about problems, they were ignored or insulted. The B.C. Ferries board was stuffed with NDP supporters and so kept quiet when questions and protests were needed.

Contracts were let on a cost-plus basis and, naturally, there were few checks on expenses. The total price of the three ferries was at first estimated to be $210 million. Final figures came in at around $463 million.

The catamarans began running in mid-1999 but rarely reached their operating speed of 40 knots, about twice the speed of a conventional ferry. After a few months, two were mothballed and one was kept to use as a spare. All were put up for sale.

While Harcourt was still finding his way around the cabinet offices, rumours had been circulating in Victoria about a scandal that would later open the door to his departure.

The "Bingogate" scandal really began when the Nanaimo Commonwealth Holding Society was formed in the 1950s as a charity to provide support for the local CCF party. After a while it

Elizabeth Cull, Glen Clark's finance minister, defends the controversial 1996 budget when questioned about an auditor general's report. Clark had claimed there would be a budgetary surplus and then called an election in which the NDP scraped home. Cull, however, lost her seat. After the election the government admitted that there would be a substantial deficit because, it said, the forecasts from government agencies were too optimistic; critics claimed the government had asked for optimistic forecasts in a ploy to win the election. The "Fudge-it Budget," provoked recall campaigns, a lawsuit and a critical auditor general's report.

started to run bingo games and was reborn as a virtual bank, with powers to lend and borrow money, and deal in real estate. Dave Stupich, Nanaimo NDP MLA, provincial cabinet member and MP, was the architect. The society sought bribes from the charities to whom it gave money and a variety of false accounts were used to hide the fraud.

Soon there were rumours about the society's actions and the way it was filtering charity money to the NDP. Shortly after Harcourt became premier, the RCMP seized the society's records. As the rumours grew, the premier, protesting the innocence of the party, ordered an audit by a private forensic accountant, Ron Parks. The society, meanwhile, had pleaded guilty to breaking gambling laws and was fined.

In 1995 the audit of the society's records exposed a massive tangle of deceptive accounting, and the fact that the NDP was getting money from the society.

Harcourt tried to evade blame for the scandal and the NDP denied getting money. But the media, his opponents in the party

July 1993: RCMP officers drag protesters from a sit-in near Clayoquot Sound on the West Coast of Vancouver Island, where they were trying to halt clear-cut logging of old-growth forests close to the inlet where Captain Cook landed in 1778. The sit-in was part of what was probably the most publicized environmental protest campaign in B.C. It lasted 15 years. Logging firms persuaded the courts to issue injunctions; protesters and their allies accused the courts of giving in too easily. Those who disobeyed the injunctions were arrested by police, not for breaking the law but for defying the court. At one time hundreds were arrested and many were jailed, including a 74-year-old woman. Robert Kennedy Jr. and other notables joined the protest, which included consumer boycott campaigns in Europe.

and the unions, who thought he was too mild and conciliatory, forced Harcourt out. In November 1995, he quit.

Three years later Stupich, 80 years old, was charged with fraud and other offences. He pleaded guilty to one fraud charge. His lawyer said his client was suffering from senile dementia, and Stupich was sentenced to two years' house arrest. Charges against two of his relatives were stayed. The court was told that about $1 million was missing.

The RCMP investigated claims that bingo money also was used to pay $80,000 to former NDP cabinet member Bob Williams to resign his Legislature seat so that Dave Barrett could run in a by-election in 1976. The police wanted charges laid, but Crown prosecutors said no crimes were involved and there would be no charges.

The leadership convention to replace Harcourt, held in February 1996, was a briskly run affair. Glen Clark easily beat Corky Evans and Joan Smallwood and moved into the premier's office on February 22.

Clark was 38. He had graduated from Simon Fraser University, gone to work in a machine shop and joined the Ironworkers

Federal Minister for Indian Affairs and Northern Development, Jane Stewart, Nisga'a Nation President Joe Gosnell and B.C.'s Premier Glen Clark celebrate the initialling of the Nisga'a Final Agreement in 1998 after years of negotiation. The agreement was later approved by Parliament and the B.C. Legislature.

Union. Later he earned an MA in urban planning at UBC, where he met Professor Tom Gunton, who was to work with him during most of his political career. In 1985 Clark was nominated as candidate in Vancouver East and a year later, he was elected to the Legislature. Five years later, he was in cabinet as finance minister.

The new premier was quickly in trouble. Clark was accused of permitting some B.C. Hydro employees, including chairman John Laxton and president John Sheehan and some NDP bigwigs to profit in a contract for a power development in Pakistan. Clark, who had been minister responsible for B.C. Hydro in the Harcourt cabinet, said he knew nothing of the contract or the financial details and had not profited in any way. He appointed Brian Smith, a cabinet minister under Bill Bennett and Bill Vander Zalm, to head Hydro and inquire into the affair, dubbed "Hydrogate."

The province's dependence on resources and its weakness when its market rival, the United States, cracked the whip were evident in the next few months when, to preserve the softwood lumber agreement, Canada agreed to cut its share of the market from 36 percent to 30. B.C. was severely affected, for its share of the

Canadian quota was 65 percent. More bad news: Ottawa announced that it would try to halve the Pacific salmon fishing fleet by buying back quotas.

But the sun came out in April, or seemed to, when Victoria brought down the budget. A small surplus was forecast for fiscal 1996–7. There'd be some small tax cuts. With what he claimed was a balanced budget in his pocket, Clark called an election for May. He won, narrowly, but this promise of a balanced budget came back to plague him for the rest of his term, sparking a rash of court cases and official inquiries and dominating provincial politics for months.

In June Finance Minister Andrew Petter reintroduced the budget, which had not been passed because of the election. He

Protesters stroll outside Premier Glen Clark's home in east Vancouver in March 1999. Soon there would be TV cameras recording an RCMP raid on the home, and Clark's time in office would be over in the hubbub over a sundeck built for him by a friend.

called for a freeze on capital spending and later admitted that instead of a $114 million surplus there would be a $200 million deficit. In July Clark said he had known there might be a deficit, but the chance was so remote that he didn't tell voters. Petter said bad weather had cut revenue from the forest industry and so spoiled the government's financial forecasting, but critics pointed out that the weather had been fine.

In September the NDP said that it would cut $750 million from expenses and 3,000 civil-service jobs over the next 18 months. A month later the government spent $115,000 to buy television time so that Premier Clark could admit that his budget forecasting was optimistic. In December Petter admitted that the deficit was now $369 million. Then the casual tossing around of words and figures stopped and the courts were consulted. B.C. Supreme Court agreed that a citizens' lawsuit alleging that the NDP had committed fraud in the election could go ahead. Critics said the argument about the budget and the election belonged in politics, not the

Lieutenant Governor Garde Gardom helps Dan Miller sign the big book at Government House in August 1999. Miller took over as interim premier after Glen Clark's resignation but told his colleagues he would not be a candidate for the job, opening the way for a leadership contest won by Ujjal Dosanjh.

courts, but the case was heard, lots of witnesses called, and the suit was dismissed. Look to politics to get redress, the complainants were told by the judge.

In December 1997, Petter said the deficit would be $352 million. Revenues from the forest sector were low.

At the beginning of 1999, another protest group tried, unsuccessfully, to overturn the results of the 1996 election, claiming the vote had been won unfairly with Clark's balanced-budget claim. On March 30, Joy McPhail, now finance minister, said the deficit for the previous financial year was $890 million. B.C.'s debt was now $34.7 billion. In 1991 it was $20 billion. The deficit had reached $1.3 billion by March 2000 when Finance Minister Paul Ramsey announced the Budget Transparency and Accountability Act, which required Victoria to balance the books by 2004.

If ever there was an election to be won just by showing up, that

Refugees from China, who have sailed across the Pacific on a decrepit small freighter, sit on the deck of a Canadian navy ship off the B.C. coast in fall 1999. Two other ships had tried to smuggle refugees into B.C., but all were caught and handed over to the authorities. Some of B.C's media treated the arrival of the starving, poor refugees as an invasion. The ships' approaches were plotted as in a scene in a war movie. The media paid little attention to reports that other countries, particularly Australia, Britain and France, were the targets of long-term, large-scale refugee smuggling. Few of the refugees stayed in Canada: many were deported; others disappeared.

of May 1996 should have been Gordon Campbell's. But he fought a poor campaign, had no clear vision for the province and could offer only negatives. However, Clark provided plenty of opportunity to make up lost ground as time passed.

In October 1996, the government announced the Vancouver Island Highway project. Its value to Island communities was apparent, but the contracting procedures guaranteed jobs for construction unions and infuriated the business community, which claimed costs were increased and Clark was helping his friends.

Environmentalists and other lovers of the outdoors were pleased in October when the government announced 23 new sites for parks. Since 1992, the NDP had created 225 parks, covering 9.3 percent of the province's land area.

Sometimes Clark did the right thing in other ways, too. He failed to cut a deal with the Americans, who were offering cash for

A Kermode bear, one of a cream-coloured subspecies of black bear, looks for food in the forest near New Aiyansh. The bears became a symbol of environmental triumph when an agreement was reached in 2000 by government, First Nations, environmentalists, logging firms and workers to protect 24 valleys in the so-called Great Bear Rainforest on the central Pacific coast of B.C. The agreement showed that the tactics of confrontation, which had governed environmental protection in the province, were slowly being superseded.

the downstream benefits earned by Premier W. A. C. Bennett's contracts from the 1960s. Instead, B.C. got a block of power that became very valuable when energy prices soared in 2001.

In April 1997, the new Forest Practices Code was announced and then came the Timber Accord. In late 1997, a Skeena Cellulose bailout saved hundreds of forestry jobs in the Prince Rupert area. The NDP started a rescue operation with money and pressure on the banks to write off some of Skeena's debts, but one bank wanted none of the deal, and the province became half-owner of Skeena.

In November 1997, the NDP faced the first of a series of challenges outside the Legislature and the normal political arena. Recall campaigns to unseat Paul Ramsey in Prince George North and Helmut Giesbrecht in Skeena began when canvassers started knocking on doors to get the requisite signatures. When the hubbub died down, Elections B.C. ruled the campaigns failures — too few signatures, it ruled.

As 1997 closed, the Legislature began debate on the controversial Nisga'a Treaty. Liberal leader Campbell said the treaty, a product of long negotiations among Ottawa, Nisga'a leaders and Victoria, threatened the Constitution because it set up a third level of government.

Ottawa had started talks with the Nisga'a in 1974. Other negotiations started, too. Ottawa and the Sechelt Nation band agreed in 1986 that the band would be granted self-government and the title to certain parcels of land.

In 1990 the Vander Zalm government joined Ottawa in negotiation with First Nations in general and the Nisga'a in particular. In 1991 Victoria said it recognized Native people's right to title and agreed to negotiate "just and fair" treaties. In 1998 Ottawa and Victoria agreed on a treaty with the Nisga'a that later passed both the Legislature and Parliament. But Liberal leader Campbell said he would challenge the treaty in various ways, and there were Native opponents of the pact: a dissident group of Nisga'a claimed the Nisga'a were not a nation but a linguistic group.

Talks continued with 10 other Native groups, and early in 2001

*S*ome measure of the resentment and fractiousness that govern politics in B.C. and make politicians' lives so turbulent can be gauged by the various recall campaigns and lawsuits begun by the populist right wing during Glen Clark's regime.

Legislation authorizing recall campaigns was passed in 1995 by the Mike Harcourt government in a flush of trust-the-people enthusiasm and after massive support in a referendum. It was the first and, so far, the only recall legislation in Canada.

The recall law was, no doubt, part of the reaction to complaints that, once elected, politicians forget their voters. But it failed to realize that many voters in B.C. and elsewhere see their MLAs and MPs as servants bound to work only for their constituency and to support the views of special-interest groups centred in the constituency. They do not see politicians as leaders or their representatives helping to govern the country or province.

The recall process, which requires 40 percent or more of the people eligible to vote at the last election to support recall, was attacked on two fronts. Some said the conditions were too stringent and made a successful recall vote impossible. Others complained that the process was open to manipulation by groups.

Eleven recall campaigns were started between 1997 and 1999, including one aimed at Gordon Campbell, then Opposition leader. None succeeded. Some were withdrawn, others failed to meet the requirements. Some MLAs faced more than one recall campaign: Paul Ramsey, education minister and finance minister and MLA for Prince George North, was challenged three times; Helmut Giesbrecht, of Skeena, twice; and Ellen Gillespie, of Comox Valley, twice.

Total Recall, a campaign aiming at a mass recall, failed. Liberal leader Campbell, perhaps realizing that recalls apply to all parties, said before the 2001 election that he would improve the process. The recall legislation helped to get rid of a dishonest MLA: Paul Reitsma, a Liberal, wrote letters to local newspapers using false names, praising himself and castigating his opponents. A recall campaign drew enough signatures, but Reitsma resigned.

Ottawa, Victoria and the Nuu-chah-nulth Tribal Council announced a tentative agreement. The group, representing the people who live on the west coast of Vancouver Island from Barkley Sound to Kyuquot Sound and whose forebears greeted Captain Cook, were to get 550 square kilometres of land, $250 million, self-government and rights to fishing and resources.

The province's doctors, angered by the failure of talks with the province about pay, equipment and patient loads, said they would soon start rotating strikes by closing offices two days a month. Doctors in the Interior had their own problems; they wanted more hospital beds, a lighter patient load and paid compensation for problems caused by isolation and few doctors.

The recession in Asia began causing problems in B.C. in the mid-1990s. Macmillan Bloedel, once a pillar of the province, claimed to have lost money for the last four quarters and was going to trim its operations. A short while later, Premier Clark announced a cut in stumpage rates — a move that threatened the lumber pact with the United States. It failed to save MacMillan Bloedel, taken over in 1999 by one of its American rivals, Weyerhaeuser.

Victoria took over casino gambling in the province by becoming the official operator of 17 casinos that shared revenues with charities. Casinos were still owned privately, but the move sidestepped the Criminal Code.

Former NDP premier Dave Barrett was appointed to lead an inquiry into the growing scandal of leaking condominiums in B.C., mainly in the Lower Mainland. Complaints about shoddy workmanship and cursory inspections were ignored by governments of all levels and suppressed by the media, but eventually the owners started suing and protesting. Barrett called for home warranties, tighter regulations, special loans and reductions in taxes to help pay for repairs, and some changes were made, but most of the improvements came as banks, builders, developers, owners and municipal inspectors realized that the building industry needed to be changed.

The B.C. Business Summit, a group of business organizations, gave its report on what it believed was wrong in B.C. It suggested tax cuts, more access to Crown land and resources, a balanced budget and reformed labour laws.

The year 1999 began with a surprise. Former Liberal leader Gordon Wilson quit as leader of the PDA and joined the NDP and cabinet in one fell swoop. His responsibilities: the B.C. Ferry Corporation and First Nations issues.

But he stepped aboard a listing, if not sinking, ship. In May an RCMP squad raided Premier Clark's home in east Vancouver while his wife and children and a camera crew looked on. The police warrant concerned a casino-licence application by a strip-club owner, Stephen Ng, and Dimitrios Pilarinos, a builder and friend of Clark's. No one could explain how the television station knew in advance about the raid.

There was no escape for Glen Clark. In August Attorney General Ujjal Dosanjh confirmed that the premier was being investigated by the RCMP and Clark resigned. His trial on breach-of-trust charges was under way in 2002.

Dan Miller took over the premier's office after assuring everyone that he would not be a candidate later for Clark's job. Ujjal Dosanjh won the leadership convention in the New Year, garnering 58 percent of the votes and romping home.

Ujjal Dosanjh, who succeeded Glen Clark as premier in 2000, was the first Indo-Canadian premier in Canada. He came to B.C. from the Punjab as a young man and was educated at Langara College, Simon Fraser University and University of British Columbia law school. After practising law in Vancouver, he was elected to the Legislature in 1991 and became attorney general in 1995.

In the first opinion polls taken after his election, Dosanjh's personal approval rating substantially outstripped his party, and some observers wondered if he could give the NDP a measure of respectability and support. He had set himself a daunting task: to govern for about a year, then call an election.

Dosanjh was soon spending. More money went to health care and education. He was helped by bigger grants from Ottawa, restoring to some extent the cuts that had crippled health care across the country earlier in the 1990s. Windfalls from energy production also meant the government could spend without getting too deeply into debt. Dosanjh's attempts to distance himself from Clark, however, took a bad fall when he was seen as mixed up in a lumber affair that was, he admitted, "a mess" and made the government "look horrible."

In 1983 Bill Bennett's forests ministry faced a problem of beetle infestation in trees on the Chilcotin plateau. The solution: persuade a forestry company to log the infected trees. The only company to agree was a Prince George firm, Carrier Lumber. By 1993 the local Native people were pressing a land claim and including the lumber. Stalling for time, the NDP government

Stockwell Day, Canadian Alliance leader, is wearing a B.C. Lions sweater as he enters the Abbotsford Tradex Centre two days before the federal election in November 2000. Day improved his party's standing in B.C. and the West, but failed in the rest of Canada. When he won the Alliance leadership he had to find a seat in the Commons: should it be in Alberta or B.C.? His staff picked B.C.'s Okanagan-Similkameen, a safe right-wing seat.

under Mike Harcourt tried to appease the First Nations by ending the ongoing contract with Carrier Lumber. (In February 2001, Harcourt said the government had wanted only to suspend the timber contract, not cancel it. He couldn't reveal this at the time, he said, because lawsuits had begun.)

Carrier, deprived of cutting about $150 million worth of timber, went to court. In July 1999, B.C. Supreme Court found in favour of Carrier and criticized the government for abusive, arrogant and illegal treatment of the company.

As Attorney General, Dosanjh had decided to appeal this judgement. As premier, he decided to abandon the appeal after documents relating to the Carrier case, but not produced in court, were found in Victoria offices. Dosanjh admitted he had not read the files properly when he ordered the appeal.

The cost? Carrier Lumber wanted $156 million, with legal costs reaching $500,000.

More pleasant and, perhaps, longer-lasting concerns: government, First Nations, environmental organizations, logging firms and, reluctantly, logging unions, agreed on a plan to protect the Great Bear Rainforest on the Pacific coast — home of Kermode bears, a strain of black bears with cream coats, that had become symbols for environmentalists of the claims of wildlife. The NDP government also banned the hunting of grizzlies to allow for surveys of their habitat and numbers.

Dosanjh called the Legislature in March, and Finance Minister Paul Ramsey brought in a budget that allocated $225 million for key projects. That left a $725 million surplus.

What's a B.C. budget without a fuss? This time critics said the government had juggled the books by taking high estimates of revenue from B.C. Hydro and the Insurance Corporation of B.C. Those moves, it was claimed, enabled the NDP to justify its spending and still have a rosy budget.

For a while after the budget the Legislature went on considering legislation, but the Liberals refused to play, calling for an election and saying they would rescind the bills passed if given the chance. Finally, on April 16, Premier Dosanjh went to see Lieutenant Governor Garde Gardom and a new era in B.C. politics began.

Twenty-eight days later, Gordon Campbell's Liberals had won a massive majority, in both seats and popular vote. Their majority in seats (77–2) was the largest since the Conservatives won 39 seats in a 42-seat House in 1912. In popular vote (more than 62 percent) it left the triumphs of the Socreds far behind. The NDP seats dropped from 39 to two, the Vancouver ridings won by Joy McPhail and Jenny Kwan. Premier Dosanjh was defeated in his Vancouver riding.

The premier had run an inept campaign and frittered away a solid personal lead in opinion polls. He campaigned almost until the end as if he would be re-elected and then, suddenly and unnecessarily, conceded victory, probably harming his own and other NDP candidates' campaigns.

In some constituencies the Liberal popular vote was more than
70 percent. That kind of figure intrigued political scientists and
other analysts, who wondered why the prosperous electorate of a
province would vote so massively against a ruling party. The mag-
nitude of the Liberals' win could endanger the parliamentary system and engender concerns about the political stability and
sophistication of voters. And given the province's history of
resentful voting against a party or individual, not for the alterna-
tive, experts wondered how much support Campbell would have
for his full program.

Adriane Carr, the new, personable leader who brought the
Green Party to life, was tipped by some as the outsider to watch,
but her dash to the post failed, though the party won 12 percent
of the popular vote. The other small parties also were overrun,
which led to the question: where and who was Her Majesty's
Loyal Opposition? When Campbell announced the structure of
the Legislature's committees, he emphasized that neither of the
two Opposition MLAs would be members.

But perhaps most significant for the future of the province was
Campbell's constant repetition of the promises made in his election manifesto — as if the election were a close-run thing and he
needed to clinch victory.

The political picture had changed and the economy had
slowed still further in the wake of the terrorist attack in the U.S.
on September 11, yet Campbell seemed to regard his campaign
rhetoric as a detailed policy blueprint. This determination would,
some experts feared, seriously hamper his plans to revitalize a dis-
heartened province.

Very quickly he was faced with major labour disputes: B.C.
Transit bus drivers were opposing partial privatization and
employment of part-time drivers at lower rates; nurses were
demanding substantial pay increases; paramedical workers such
as pharmacists also sought more. He declared teachers an essential service and legislated them back to work when they with-
held voluntary services. He delivered massive cuts to the civil

Premier Gordon Campbell addresses the Vancouver Board of Trade in November 2001. Born in 1948 to a wealthy, talented, well-connected Vancouver family, Campbell was educated in Vancouver and then went to Dartmouth College, an American post-secondary school. After teaching for two years in Nigeria and a short spell at UBC law school, he became Vancouver Mayor Art Phillips' executive assistant and then returned to UBC to earn an MBA. From 1976 to 1986 he was a developer, became a Non-Partisan Association Vancouver city councillor in 1983 and mayor in 1986. After two terms he switched to provincial politics; he was elected Liberal leader in 1993 and premier in 2001.

service and ended funding of many public programs.

In trying to fulfill three important promises — to revive the economy, to hold a referendum on the terms of negotiation of First Nations land claims and to open up government — he faced, severe problems. These were caused not only by the province's vulnerability to external economic forces, but also by the constitution and the local political climate. As well, he had to confront the old issues of forestry, the fishery, pollution of the air, land and water, use of the land and care of wildlife. Once, we could treat them seriously. No longer — by the 1990s it had become clear that there was only one big issue: how could the people of B.C. live to the full and yet do the least damage to the land, sea, water

The scene here is on Granville Street in Vancouver, but it could be anywhere in B.C.: a movie crew is preparing to shoot a scene as the light fades and the rain starts. By 2002 some $1.2 billion was being contributed annually to the provincial economy by the movie industry.

and air, fish and animals? This question is the battle cry of environmental groups and their sympathizers. B.C. has been a fertile home for them since the 1950s, and many a fight they have won.

But by 1995, for all intents and purposes the battles were over, although some sustainable logging continued in agreed areas. In the late 1990s, Prime Minister Jean Chretien celebrated Clayoquot's designation as an international biosphere reserve. By 2001 the pattern seemed to be set: all the participants recognized that some compromises were necessary.

Environmental dangers lurked in the metropolitan areas, too, but there were few protests. A dangerous haze caused by vehicles and industry hung over Greater Vancouver and the Fraser Valley when climatic conditions favoured it. Attempts to cut automobile traffic were feeble and slow. Sewage systems were inadequate. Urban planning, both for practical and aesthetic purposes, often was minimal. Sometimes developers and planners combined to create the urban equivalent of clearcut logging — vast areas of large homes without trees, shade or green space.

This book's story began when the people of British Columbia lived in a closed fishing and hunting society, based on a mystical relationship with the natural world. All that changed when the explorers and settlers came and built cities, logged the forests, fished the ocean, dug mines and traded with the world. Hundreds of years later, British Columbians are facing equally massive changes to their lives. Big government and a prosperous economy, largely based on exploiting the once abundant natural resources of the province, are in question. As well, the province is trying to determine its relationship with the world far beyond its borders, rapidly changing and controlled — it often seems — by economic, ideological and technological forces beyond its control.

B.C.'s fishing industry is bedevilled by constitutional, racial and bureaucratic wrangling. Here fishermen, angered by closures ordered by the Department of Fisheries and Oceans, cast their lines in protest in 1997 — but do not actually fish. Officials claimed they were still breaking regulations.

Our final excerpt, from The Last Great Sea, *takes us away from city sophistication and back to essentials — wind, sea, land, people and how they work together. Terry Glavin has researched and written about the fishery, Native people, the environment and the ocean for many years as both journalist and scientific writer.*

For most people, Mayne Island is a picturesque landfall on the ferry trip from Tsawwassen to Vancouver Island; for Terry Glavin and his friends, the crab fishers, however, the island is the centre around which their working lives revolve. Officialdom may chart the fishing areas, but for Glavin and his friends the map is full of mysteries.

Back home on Mayne Island, where I live, there is a certain crab fisherman by the name of Bob Strain. There are days when it's cold and pouring rain and there's nothing much to look forward to except sliding around the deck of the *Lorna Doone* pulling line after line of crab traps from a choppy sea while the boat heaves and shudders and you ache to your very bones by the time you're headed back to Horton Bay. And there are mornings when the whole world is sleeping, and the early-morning canopy of gray cloud dangles in the upper limbs of the arbutus and the cedar, and there is no sound, and nothing moves, except a single chattering kingfisher that plunges into the shallows now and then after a sandlance or a pipefish. A voice crackles on the marine radio, something about rippled seas and something about scattered rain somewhere, but nothing scatters from Campbell Point to Potato Point, and nothing ripples, and far out into the gulf, the sea is calm and fat and languorous.

There are the necessary mysteries. Horton Bay bites into Mayne Island's southeast side, behind Curlew Island, and Bob puts out in the *Lorna Doone* to the places he sets his lines of traps, but to disclose where his traps are would be to violate a necessary rule of so many fisheries. You don't tell the world where your favorite fishing spots are. It's just not done.

There is also the mystery of place. It is true enough to say that Bob fishes in an area that Fisheries and Oceans knows as the southern section of the Gulf Islands quadrant on the crab-license charts known as Area H. I know the area as a place bordered by Curlew Island, which is infested with feral peacocks, and off the southern point of Curlew my son Eamonn caught his first rockfish. Older islanders might put the northern tip of Bob's fishing grounds at the spot where Harold Payne used to beach his little sailboat at Bennett Bay, in the 1890s, in the days when old Harold would sail up from Saturna Island, rain or shine, to collect the mail. Some of the older Tsartlip people, whose ancestors have known these waters from time out of mind, might identify the place marking the northern extent of Bob's crab traps as the site where the Tsartlips killed and buried a certain wicked man, hundreds of years ago, after the man had mistreated his brother's slaves by using their bodies as canoe skids.

There is the mystery of ways and means. Bob's boat is the *Lorna Doone*, a 37-foot lobster boat from Newcastle, New Brunswick, and nobody knows how it found its way to this coast. It's known to have been around the Gulf Islands since the 1950s...

The *Lorna Doone* is one of only about 220 crab-licensed boats coast-wide, and the crab fishery is puny compared with the herring fishery or salmon fishery, and it is a reasonable and defensible fishery. It's a live-capture fishery. It's not only species-selective but selective by size and gender as well. It's managed by DFO scientists who are not so inflated by hubris that they cannot admit that there are mysteries about things, and there are mysteries about Dungeness crab, otherwise known as Cancer magister.

Bob insists, for instance, that there are "resident" crabs, which are gnarly and barnacle encrusted and don't appear to leave their own little bays, and there are "runs" of crabs, like salmon runs. Bob also observes that you can haul traps all day on the Plumper Sound side of Mayne Island and all you'll get is females, which, by regulation, have to go back in the water. But on the gulf side, the crabs are almost always males, which, if they are 165 millimeters (6½ inches) across the back, are "keepers." There's one spot on the gulf side where the crabs have their own distinctive reddish color about their legs and pincers. Bob says there is a highway out there on the sea bottom, and if you're lucky enough to set a line of traps on top of it the traps will be full to bursting with big, beautiful Dungeness, but if you miss it by a couple of boat lengths your traps will come up empty. And the highway is always moving. So it's mysterious, but it is also quite maddening.

Dates to Remember

11,000 years ago: Hunters in Interior B.C.

9,000 years ago: Native people on coast.

1579: Sir Francis Drake sails into North Pacific.

1774: First Spanish exploration.

1778: Captain Cook arrives in Friendly Cove.

1779: Spanish follow Cook.

1792: Captain Vancouver starts mapping coast.

1793: Mackenzie reaches Pacific at Bella Coola.

1808: Fraser reaches Pacific.

1827: Fort Langley built.

1843: Fort Victoria built.

1846: Border with United States fixed at 49th Parallel

1849: Vancouver Island created a crown colony.

1858: Fraser gold rush begins.

1858: New Caledonia becomes British Columbia.

1866: Colonies of Vancouver Island and British Columbia unite.

1867: Confederation of Canada formed.

1871: Terms of union with Canada approved.

1880: Work on B.C. section of Canadian Pacific Railway begins.

1885: Last Spike driven home at Craigellachie.

1886: City of Vancouver incorporated: burns down two months later.

1898: Yukon gold rush.

1903: Richard McBride named premier; party politics begin.

1914: War with Germany.

1918: CPR's *Princess Sophia* sinks; 346 die.

1938: Jobless take over Vancouver Post Office, Art Gallery and Hotel Georgia.

1939: Canada declares war on Germany.

1941: Liberal-Conservative coalition formed.

1952: W. A. C. Bennett becomes premier.

1953: Massive road-building program begins.

1967: Duncan dam on Columbia built.

1972: NDP's Dave Barrett wins election

1975: Bill Bennett leads Socreds back to power.

1982: Restraint program begins.

1986: Bill Bennett resigns; Bill Vander Zalm takes over.

1991: Vander Zalm resigns; Socreds name Rita Johnston premier.

1991: Mike Harcourt wins election for NDP.

1992: Recall legislation introduced.

1994: Fast ferry plan announced.

1995: Harcourt resigns; audit reveals Bingo scandal.

1996: New premier Glen Clark calls election after promising a balanced Budget.

1997: Recall campaigns start.

1998: Nisga'a treaty approved in Victoria and Ottawa.

1999: RCMP raid Clark's home: he resigns.

2000: Ujjal Dosanjh becomes premier.

2001: Gordon Campbell's Liberals win runaway election.

Other Books About British Columbia

Akrigg, G.P.V. and Helen Akrigg. *British Columbia Chronicle, 1778-1846 and 1847-1871* Two vols. Vancouver: Discovery Press 1977.

> Interesting, gossipy accounts of life in early B.C.

Barman, Jean. *The West Beyond the West: A History of British Columbia.* Toronto: University of Toronto 1991.

> The definitive history of the province. Full of information, but a little boring when Barman rides her hobby-horses.

Berton, Pierre. *The Last Spike: the Great Railway 1881-1885.* Toronto: McClelland and Stewart 1971.

— *The Great Depression 1929-1939.* Toronto: McClelland and Stewart 1990.

> Both popular histories by the Canadian master. The railway history somehow fails to convey the excitement of the struggle to conquer a wild continent but the account of the Depression, with its stories of courage and blind, official stupidity, is first-rate.

Bowering, George. *Bowering's B.C.: a Swashbuckling History.* Toronto: Viking, 1996.

> Poet and novelist Bowering gives his version of the province's history. Witty, irreverent and intent on defending the First Nations' cause.

Brody, Hugh. *Maps and Dreams: Indians and the British Columbia Frontier.* Vancouver: Douglas & McIntyre 1981

> Brody, British sociologist, writer and film-maker, lived with First Nations people in northern B.C and wrote this intriguing account of hunters who use dreams to find their quarry.

Coupland, Douglas. *City of Glass.* Vancouver: Douglas & McIntyre 2000.

An illustrated grab-bag — sometimes exasperating, never dull — of Coupland's writing. As Brody illustrates life in the B.C. Interior, Coupland shines a light on the actions and thoughts of B.C.'s metropolis.

Fisher, Robin. *Contact and Conflict: Indian-European Relations in British Columbia.* Vancouver: UBC Press 1977.

Written nearly 30 years ago, Fisher's book is still essential reading for anyone trying to make sense of the relations between First Nations people and the settlers.

— Johnston H. eds. *Captain Cook and his Times.* Vancouver: Douglas & McIntyre 1979.

A collection of writing about Cook, his navy, seamen, government and his achievements.

Fladmark, Knut. *British Columbia Prehistory.* Ottawa: National Museum of Man 1986.

BC.'s history from the Year One, as told by archaeology. Fladmark has assembled the evidence about early life in B.C. but sometimes lets his enthusiasm overpower his good sense.

Francis, Daniel ed. *The Encyclopedia of British Columbia.* Madeira Park: Harbour 2000.

A first-rate achievement and a wonderful resource for anyone who wants to know more about the province.

Glavin, Terry. *The Last Great Sea.* Vancouver: Greystone Books 2000.

All you need to know about the Pacific Ocean - its past, future and the people and creatures who live in it and on its shores - by a writer, fisherman and researcher.

Hoover, Alan. Ed. *Nuu-chah-nulth Voices, Histories, Objects and Journeys.* Victoria: Royal British Columbia Museum 2000.

> The First Nations people who live on the west coast of Vancouver Island give their version of west coast history.

Kitagawa, Muriel. *This is My Own.* Vancouver: Talonbooks 1985.

> An excellent source of information about the deportation of B.C.'s Japanese Canadians. Here are articles by Kitagawa, letters to her brother, photographs and an introduction by Roy Miki.

Mackie, Richard Somerset. *Island Timber.* Victoria: Sono Nis Press 2000.

> A model for historians: an illustrated account of how one company logged vast tracts of Vancouver Island - with the details, stories and themes that transform a collection of facts into a history.

Mair, Rafe. *Rants, Raves and Recollections.* Vancouver: Whitecap 2000.

> Read it for the recollections of life in Vancouver in the Forties.

Mason, Gary and Keith Baldrey. *Fantasyland.* Toronto: McGraw Hill 1989.

> Two reporters tell the Vander Zalm story.

Mitchell, David. *Succession: the Political Reshaping of British Columbia.* Vancouver: Douglas & McIntyre 1987.

— *W.A.C.: Bennett and the Rise of British Columbia.* Vancouver: Douglas & McIntyre 1983.

> Well-researched, these two books tell the story of the Bennetts - father William Andrew Cecil and son Bill.

Persky, Stan. *Son of Socred.* Vancouver: New Star 1979.

— *Bennett II.* Vancouver: New Star 1987

More about Bill Bennett and his reign.

— *Fantasy Government: Bill Vander Zalm and the Future of Social Credit.* Vancouver: New Star: 1989.

More about Vander Zalm. Persky's books, detailed, very readable, present a view of B.C. politics well to the left of conventional political thought.

Reksten, Terry. *The Illustrated History of British Columbia.* Vancouver: Douglas & McIntyre 2001.

A sumptuous book, to be treasured for the illustrations.

Resnick, Philip. *The Politics of Resentment: B.C.: Regionalism and Canadian Unity.* Vancouver: UBC Press 2000.

Resnick charts and describes B.C.'s hostility to central Canada and tries to explain it.

Robin, Martin. *The Rush for Spoils: The Company Province 1871-1933.* Toronto: McClelland & Stewart 1972.

— *Pillars of Profit: The Company Province 1934-1972.* Toronto: McClelland & Stewart 1973.

Anyone trying to describe or understand politics and business in B.C. must read,carefully,Robin's books, written 30 years ago.

Sherman, Paddy. *Bennett.* Toronto: McClelland & Stewart 1963.

Sherman was one of the reporters who covered Bennett's reign of B.C. with expertise, good sense and judgment.

Sobel, Dava. *Longitude: The True Story of a Lone Genius Who Solved the Greatest Scientific Problem of his Time*. New York: Walker 1993.

> The genius was John Harrison. The problem: how can a ship's master determine his position when he is in mid-ocean?

Stouck, David and Myler Wilkison eds. *Genius of Place*. Vancouver: Polestar 2000.

> A collection of writing about B.C. from John Jewitt (1815) to Bill Richardson (1997).

Twigg, Alan: *Vander Zalm: From Immigrant to Premier*. Madeira Park: Harbour 1986.

> Still more about Vander Zalm — chatty and very readable.

White, Howard, ed. *Raincoast Chronicles*. Madeira Park: Harbour 1976–1994.

> Tales of life on the west coast.

Woodcock, George. *British Columbia: A History of the Province*. Vancouver: Douglas & McIntyre 1990.

> Should be read with Barman's history — each makes up for the other's deficiency.

Websites Concerned with British Columbia

There's plenty of information about B.C. on the Internet. But websites, unlike books, can change or vanish in a trice — so here are some major sites, as permanent as can be, which can expand, or update, the material in this book. Most sites are portals — they are gates that open to a wide range of other sites. So click on one, say, www.gov.bc.ca and you will find links to sites about statistics, business, aboriginal affairs, the premier's office and others.

Beware! Some sites are very easy to use; others seem to have been designed by a mad puzzle-maker.

B.C. government: www.gov.bc.ca
B.C. statistics: www.bcstats.gov.bc.ca
B.C. Ministry of Aboriginal Affairs: www.gov.bc.ca/aaf
Canadian government: www.gc.ca/main_e
Canadian statistics: www.statcan.ca (cct)
University of B.C. Library: www.library.ubc.ca
Vancouver Public Library: www.vpl.vancouver.bc.ca
Encyclopedia of British Columbia: www2.mybc.com/learning/ebc

Acknowledgements

Many people helped to produce this book. Here are some of them: Derek Fairbridge, Michelle Benjamin, Kevin Williams and Ana Torres. The staffs of: B.C. Archives and Records Service; Vancouver Public Library; Vancouver City Archives; University of B.C. Special Collections; British Columbia Hydro; British Columbia Ferry Corporation; British Columbia Ministry of Tourism; Royal British Columbia Museum; and the Pacific Newspaper Group Library (particularly Kate Bird and Sandra Boutilier).

Photo Credits

BCARS: B.C. Archives and Records Service
CM: Cumberland Museum
CVA: Vancouver City Archives

PNG: Pacific Newspaper Group
RBCM: Royal British Columbia Museum
VPL: Vancouver Public Library

Front Cover:
BCARS A-01782

Back Cover:
clockwise from top left
BCARS A-02678
BCARS A-2037
VPL 1380
PNG
PNG
PNG

Chapter One:
p.4	BCARS A-02678
p.6	BCARS PDP04222
p.9	PDP022252
p.10	BCARS A-02312
p.12	CVA BO-P.1, N.3
p.13	BCARS A-01229
p.14	CVA OUT-P.520, N.201
p.15	BCARS PDP02612
p.16	BCARS A-08953
p.18	BCARS A-01722
p.19	BCARS CM/A-78
p.20	BCARS C-06124
p.21	BCARS A-03081
p.22	BCARS G-05497
p.24	BCARS A-01514
p.25	B-02767
p.26	RBCM PN4648

Chapter Two:
p.30	BCARS A-03988
p.31	CVA OUT-P.959, N.511
p.32	VPL 8690
p.34	VPL 19928
p.35	CVA IN-P.87, N.158
p.37	BCARS D-07548
p.38	VPL 7779
p.40	CVA CAN-P.218, N.224
p.41	VPL 391
p.42	BCARS E-02200
p.43	CVA 3-4 (F. Dally)
p.44	BCARS A-01321
p.45	BCARS D-06674
p.46	CVA CAN-P.2, N.56
p.47	CVA WAT-P.3, N.10
p.48	VPL 13246
p.49	VPL 2249
p.50	CVA BO-P.154, N.44
p.51	VPL 5590
p.52	BCARS G-04477
p.53	(left)CVA 260-1067
p.53	(right) BCARS E-5059
p.54	BCARS A-2037

Chapter Three:
p.76	CVA STR-P.336, N.307
p.60	VPL 509
p.61	VPL 27807
p.62	CVA 196-1
p.63	BCARS H-06815
p.66	CM

Chapter Four:
p.86	BCARS F-0559
p.87	BCARS H-05389
p.89	BCARS F-09387
p.90	BCARS E-06844
p.92	BCARS I-28090
p.95	PNG
p.97	BCARS H-05392
pp.98-107	PNG

Chapter Five:
pp.110-141	PNG
p.142	Mandelbrot

p.67	VPL 1786
p.68	CVA PORT-P.817
p.69	PNG
p.70	VPL 11023
p.71	CVA 371-119
p.72	CVA BU-P.403, N.387
p.73	VPL 136
p.74	VPL 2639
p.75	BCARS C-01754;
p.76	BCARS C-07293;
p.77	VPL 2022
p.78	VPL 13338
p.79	BCARS D-09786
p.80	VPL 1277
p.81	(left) CVA OUT-P.1027
p.81	(right) PNG
p.82	VPL 1380

Author

Geoffrey Molyneux came to British Columbia after serving in the Royal Air Force and working on Fleet Street newspapers. He has been a journalist, teacher, civil servant and a Research Director in the House of Commons.

Index

A Pour of Rain: Stories from a West Coast Fort • Helen Meilleur
This reissue of an out-of-print treasure of BC history is one of the best histories we have of a West Coast community. Port Simpson is located just south of the Nass River, an area largely inhabited by the Nisga'a people. In the 1920s, Meilleur attended a one-room school on the Native reservation here, where her father ran the general store. *A Pour of Rain* combines personal memoir with a well-researched, carefully reconstructed history of the fort in the mid-nineteenth century.
1-55192-422-6 • $24.95 CDN/$18.95 US

Cabin at Singing River • Chris Czjakowski • Foreword by Peter Gzowski
This redesigned new edition of a classic account of frontier life presents the story of how one woman accomplished the task of making a slight, human indentation in a remote and uninhabited place. In her late thirties, with only rudimentary carpentry skills, Chris headed into the interior of British Columbia and, in the pristine wilderness of Tweedsmuir Provincial Park, cleared a piece of land and built her own home.
1-55192-463-3 • $21.95 CDN/$15.95 US

Hiking on the Edge (Revised Third Edition) • Ian Gill, photographs by David Nunuk
A journey in pictures and words along the West Coast Trail. With a revised section on the Juan de Fuca Marine Trail and updated information, this book is the definitive resource for both the armchair traveller and veteran hiker interested in venturing to the western edge of British Columbia's Vancouver Island.
155192-505-2 • $29.95 CDN/$19.95 US